**Edwin Lincoln Moseley (1865-1948)
Science Teacher, Sandusky High School.**

(Taken sometime before 1898; Sandusky Library Archives)

Edwin Lincoln Moseley (1865-1948), a college professor with an eccentric personality, developer of original teaching methodologies, and a keen observer as a scientific investigator, was a man of diverse interests who garnered the attention of popular writers and newspaper reporters. Moseley was a frequent subject of magazine and newspaper articles, and via these media, his popularity and fame spread widely. During the 1940's, Paul W. Jones of the Bowling Green State University news bureau continually wrote and distributed press releases about the man's unusual peculiarities and scientific research. The University, itself, was responsible for his popularity, while at the same time the institution gained wide recognition as a growing research University moving toward shedding its teacher college image.

Published in the Year of the Bicentennial of the State of Ohio

BIBLIOGRAPHY AND ARCHIVAL GUIDE

TO THE WRITINGS

OF EDWIN LINCOLN MOSELEY

Compiled By

Ronald L. Stuckey

The Ohio State University
Herbarium, Museum of Biological Diversity

With the Assistance of Relda E. Niederhofer
Bowling Green State University, Firelands College

2003

BIBLIOGRAPHY AND ARCHIVAL GUIDE TO THE WRITINGS OF EDWIN LINCOLN MOSELEY

Compiled By Ronald L. Stuckey
With the Assistance of Relda E. Niederhofer

Volume Three of a Series: Stuckey's Contributions to the Lake Erie Area of Northern Ohio.

Volume One in this Series (although not identified) is *Edwin Lincoln Moseley (1865-1948), Naturalist, Scientist, Educator*, published in 1998 by RLS Creations.

Volume Two in this Series is *Lost Stories: Yesterday and Today at Put-in-Bay, Including Theresa Thorndale's "Island Jottings" of the 1890's*, published in 2002 by RLS Creations.

Citation: Ronald L. Stuckey. 2003. Bibliography and Archival Guide to the Writings of Edwin Lincoln Moseley. RLS Creations, Columbus, Ohio. x, 84 pp.

This publication (OHSU-BS-012) was supported in part from the Ohio Sea Grant College Program and the F. T. Stone Laboratory, The Ohio State University.

Written, Compiled, Designed, Edited, and Published by:
Ronald L. Stuckey
RLS Creations
Box 12455 Columbus, Ohio 43212-0455

Computer page layout by Ricki C. Herdendorf, EcoSphere Associates
Garfield Farms, 4921 Detroit Road, Sheffield Village, Ohio 44054

Printed by Thomson-Shore, Inc.
7300 West Joy Road, Dexter, Michigan 48130

Copyright @ 2003 by Ronald L. Stuckey

ISBN 0-9668034-6-9

Introductory Commentary

Edwin Lincoln Moseley (1865-1948), a pioneer in outdoor natural science education, taught students science at Sandusky High School from 1889 to 1914 in Sandusky, Ohio. Between 1914 and his retirement in 1936, and until his death in 1948, Moseley served Bowling Green State Normal College, now Bowling Green State University, as its first professor of science. His title was truly accurate for he was a one-man science department and member of the institution's original faculty. Here he taught all of the sciences and some related subjects, including astronomy, biology, chemistry, geography, geology, hygiene, physics, philosophy, and sometimes courses in English, Latin, and geometry. Within these disciplines, Moseley conducted original research and reported what he learned to students, professional scientists, and the general public. These efforts were achieved by making presentations at meetings of scientific organizations, by giving lectures to students and general audiences, and by publishing the results of his efforts in a multitude of scientific journals, popular magazines, and local newspapers.

This book, *A Bibliography and Archival Guide to the Writings of Edwin Lincoln Moseley*, is an attempt to list all of the known written contributions, as well as those of other authors, who wrote about or interpreted Moseley's writings to professional scientists in journals or to the general public in magazines or newspapers. The bibliography as compiled here, therefore, contains more than only the writings by Moseley. To separate his writings from those articles written about Moseley and his work, the initials **ELM** in bold type appear at the end of those citations that are his. Articles written by others, if known, have their names added, but not in bold type, at the end of the reference citation. Those references lacking authors' names are considered to have been written anonymously.

Copies of nearly all of these writings by and about Moseley and his work have been assembled by Ronald L. Stuckey as an archival file deposited in the manuscript collection at the Rutherford B. Hayes Presidential Center, 1337 Hayes Avenue, Fremont, Ohio 43420-2796. A Guide to these Archives is outlined following the Bibliography in this Book, and access to them is available by contacting the Curator of Manuscripts at the Hayes Center. A Biographical Sketch of Moseley follows the Archival Guide.

Organization of the Bibliography

Moseley's Bibliography is organized into three major Sections: Scientific Contributions, Other Contributions, and Biographical Sources. Within each of these Sections, the components are subdivided further.

Moseley's Scientific Contributions are divided into nine disciplines: I. Astronomy, II. Botany, III. Geology, IV. Health and Hygiene, V. Medical Science, VI. Meteorology, VII. Ornithology, VIII. Science Education and General Science, and IX. Zoology (other than Ornithology). The components in the Section Other Contributions are: I. Essays on Various Topics, including Travel, Other Topics, and Opinions and Editorials, II. Lists of Special Lectures, III. Titles of Papers Presented at Scientific Meetings, IV. List of Local Field Excursions, V. The High School Museum at Sandusky, later moved to Bowling Green, and a VI. List of Writings in Manuscript about Moseley by Ronald L. Stuckey. The Third Section brings together the Biographical Sources written about Moseley, which are further subdivided into: I. Sketches, Commentaries, and Stories, II. Obituaries, and III. Will and Estate.

Guide to the Archives

A Guide to the Archives of the Writings of Edwin Lincoln Moseley comprises the second major component of this Book. These archives are arranged into various topics including the content and sequence of the chapters in the book, *Edwin Lincoln Moseley (1865-1948), Naturalist, Scientist, Educator* by Relda E. Niederhofer and Ronald L. Stuckey (1998). Each topic and/or chapter is assigned a Stuckey Archival Number. These numbers and their topical descriptions comprise the main guide to the Archives. The Archival Number that corresponds to each component in the bibliography is placed at the top of the page opposite each bibliographic title.

A second component to the Archival Guide is a list of individuals whose names appear in the Moseley Book by Niederhofer and Stuckey (1998). With each person's name is given his/her birth and death years, if known, and the assigned Stuckey Archival Number. This Archival File provides biographical information about these individuals accessible at the Hayes Center.

Moseley's Biographical Sketch

The third part of this Book is a biographical sketch of Edwin Lincoln Moseley (1865-1948) written by Ivan E. "Doc" Lake. Because of his careful concern for accuracy, Moseley preferred him as his biographer to any other newspaper writer. This statement came from a letter that Moseley's niece, Mrs. Pearl Ideler of Prospect, Kentucky, wrote to her children at the time of her uncle Edwin's death (Niederhofer and Stuckey, 1998, p. 210).

To preserve Mr. Lake's biographical articles of Moseley, two of them that are known, are combined into one account and reprinted here with editorial modifications. Both appeared in the Bowling Green newspaper, the *Daily Sentinel-Tribune*, the first in 1937 at the time of Moseley's retirement from teaching, and the second in 1948 at the time of Moseley's death. The biographical sketch is followed on page 84 by an editorial about Moseley's life, also written at the time of his death by the editor of the *Daily Sentinel-Tribune*.

Moseley's Achievements in Scholarship

An investigator's contributions and achievements in scholarship can be measured after compiling an inventory of those published and unpublished components of that effort. In addition, these inventories are valuable for future researchers who intend to verify and expand upon the individual's studies. Analyses of Moseley's contributions to science were published by Stuckey in the Book about Moseley by Niederhofer and Stuckey (1998, Chapters 9,10,11). These analyses were summarized there in two tables, and they are reprinted here on pages 38-41. The numbers of publications by Moseley for each discipline in the Table on page 38 have been revised according to the numbers of citations published in this bibliography. Only those publications identified with the initials **ELM** in bold type were used in determining these numbers. Moseley's largest number of publications was in Ornithology, a total of 34, followed by Meteorology and Zoology, each with 22. His most lengthy and sustained scientific interest was in Ornithology, which began in 1887 with his first publication, being a compilation of the birds and mammals in the Kent Scientific Institute, and ended with his last publication in 1947 on variations in the bird populations in the north-central states. Moseley's concentrated investigations in meteorology from 1935 to 1948 occupied a 13-year span in the latter part of his life, when he was making detailed studies of tree-ring widths and lake-level records, from which he derived rainfall cycles and made long-range weather forecasts. In this endeavor, Moseley became widely known in the popular press for his successful weather predictions. Within each scientific discipline, Moseley wrote at least one major paper, comprehensive monograph, or book. As an aid to their identification, the title pages of these comprehensive studies are placed as a frontispiece opposite the beginning page of each of the scientific bibliographies. The exception is Health and Hygiene for which no major publication was prepared.

Stuckey's Interest in Moseley

My interest in Moseley has been an informative study during my entire professional life. Having grown up in northern Ohio, my mother, Leora Irene (Shuey) Stuckey (1903-1966), who attended Bowling Green State Normal College during 1920-1922, often spoke of Moseley. Although I do not recall her saying that she had any classes with him, examination of her grade record reveals that she took a class in geography which was one of the courses that Moseley taught.

I first became aware of Moseley as a botanist when in the early summer of 1959 I attended the Franz Theodore Stone Laboratory on Gibraltar Island in Lake Erie, while an advanced undergraduate student from Heidelberg College. At the Laboratory, I studied Field Botany, a course taught by Dr. T. Richard Fisher, plant taxonomist of the Department of Botany and Plant Pathology, The Ohio State University. Reference to Moseley was made from time to time in the course, both orally and from the literature.

My interest in Moseley was heightened further, when soon after coming to The Ohio State University in 1965, I began studying his "Sandusky Flora" (1899) in connection with my research on the terrestrial flora of the islands in Lake Erie, and on the changes in the aquatic and wetland flora in and along the shoreline of Lake Erie. I also became intrigued with the diversity of scientific disciplines in which Moseley wrote papers, and consequently I began assembling a bibliography of his scientific papers and books.

Information Sources and Acknowledgements

My idea to prepare a comprehensive bibliography of the writings by and about Edwin Lincoln Moseley came during the 1960's at the same time that I had envisioned writing about his scientific achievements. The bibliography itself had its beginning in the spring of 1967, when with my brother, Darwin Wendell Stuckey, who was then a graduate student in chemistry at Bowling Green State University, helped me obtain information from the campus library. Among the items seen was a copy of Moseley's *Bibliography* compiled by Hubert Porter Stone (1952, p. 65) which contained a short list of 38 titles. I then followed by searching for more publications and by 1970 the list totaled 95 citations. Since that time I have had considerable help from librarians and friends in Bowling Green, Columbus, Fremont, Sandusky, and Toledo, who have provided me access to materials relevant to Moseley's life and accomplishments. In the fall of 1981, I prepared a four-page typewritten summary of Moseley's life and scientific achievements for a *Biographical Dictionary*, and after revision in 1996, it appeared in editor Keir B. Sterling's 1997 *Biographical Dictionary of American and Canadian Naturalists and Environmentalists*, Greenwood Press, Westport, Connecticut. In December 1998, Relda E. Niederhofer and I published our 292-page book, *Edwin Lincoln Moseley (1865-1948): Naturalist, Scientist, Educator.*

The most important and most extensive contribution to Moseley's bibliography is an *Index* to writings by and about him that appeared in the Sandusky, Ohio, newspapers, principally the *Sandusky Register*. This *Index* was prepared by Charles E. Frohman (1901-1976), a Sandusky lawyer, businessman, and local historian, who had been a high school student of Moseley. During the 1970's he wrote pamphlet-type books on Sandusky history that included short articles about Moseley's scientific work. Perhaps Frohman's least known contribution to Moseley's legacy is the *Moseley Newspaper Index* retained in the Frohman Collection at the Rutherford B. Hayes Presidential Center, Fremont, Ohio. The *Index* from the Sandusky newspapers has 170 titles, spanning a 70-year period from 1889 through 1959. From other newspapers in Erie County, Frohman indexed 78 articles.

Frohman's *Index* is of utmost importance because without it the book on Moseley's life by Niederhofer and Stuckey (1998) and my comprehensive *Bibliography and Archival Guide to the Writings of Edwin Lincoln Moseley* (this book) could not have been compiled and published. Copies of many of the articles listed in the *Frohman Index* were made from the microfilms of the Sandusky newspapers in The Ohio Historical Society, Columbus, by my former student, W. Louis Phillips, C. G. These copies are retained in the archives of the Niederhofer-Stuckey Moseley book at the Hayes Presidential Center.

I have obtained additional bibliographic citations from appropriate files in the Rutherford B. Hayes Presidential Center, the Sandusky Library, and the Toledo Public Library. The author has seen on microfilm articles in various newspapers and has verified them in the above libraries, as well as in the Tiffin and Seneca County Public Library and the Library of the Ohio Historical Society, Columbus. The author also has identified published articles in popular and scientific periodicals in the Marston Science Library, University of Florida, Gainesville, and the Biological Sciences and Pharmacy Library and other libraries of The Ohio State University, Columbus.

Relda E. Niederhofer supplied copies of articles pertaining to Moseley from the Sandusky and Erie County newspapers in the Sandusky Public Library and from the *Daily Sentinel-Tribune* (Bowling Green), the *Bowling Green State University Magazine*, and the *Bee Gee News* in the Center for Archival Collections of the Jerome Library of Bowling Green State University. She also contributed and compiled the reference citations for Moseley's Museum in the Sandusky High School, which later was transferred to Bowling Green State University. Several other individuals also have contributed articles cited in the Bibliography. Included among these are William R. Burk, Jane L. Forsyth, Harold F. Mayfield, Tom Stockdale, Edward G. Voss, and the late Eleanor Durr and Hazel Stockdale, .

Kathy Royer of the Museum of Biological Diversity, The Ohio State University, word-processed the initial drafts of the Bibliography, beginning in the early 1990's, and Andrea (Wilson) Schlageter, former secretary for the F. T. Stone Laboratory on South Bass Island, word processed a revised version in 2000. Ricki C. Herdendorf prepared the final word-processed copy of the written text and bibliographic citations in addition to the layout of the pages for the printing process. Charles E. Herdendorf has been a critical advisor and informant during the final stages of design and page preparation. My thanks is extended to all of the above mentioned individuals for their support and help. An apologetic note is added for those whose names have been overlooked, forgotten, or never recorded.

Ronald L. Stuckey

26 February 2002

TABLE OF CONTENTS

INTRODUCTORY COMMENTARY .... Ronald L. Stuckey iii
TABLE OF CONTENTS viii
SCIENTIFIC CONTRIBUTIONS
    I.   Contributions to Astronomy 1
    II.   Contributions to Botany 3
    III.   Contributions to Geology 7
    IV.   Contributions to Health and Hygiene 13
    V.   Contributions to Medical Science 17
    VI.   Contributions to Meteorology 19
    VII.   Contributions to Ornithology 25
    VIII.   Contributions to Science Education and General Science 31
    IX.   Contributions to Zoology (Other than Ornithology) 35
TABLES
    Numbers and Years of Publication for Each Discipline
        in Books and Archival Periodicals 38
    Membership in Professional Scientific Organizations
        and Summation of Publications in Periodicals 39
OTHER CONTRIBUTIONS
    I.   Essays on Various Topics 43
        A. Travels 43
        B. Other Topics 44
        C. Opinions and Editorials 44
    II.   Lists of Special Lectures 45
        A. Delivered at the Sandusky High School 45
        B. Delivered at Various Locations 46

III.	Titles of Papers Presented at Scientific Meetings	47
	A. Meetings of The Ohio Academy of Science	47
	1. Titles of Papers Presented and Published (1894-1939)	47
	2. List of Moseley's Reports as Secretary (1895-1904)	52
	B. Meetings of The Michigan Academy of Science, Arts, and Letters	53
	C. Meetings of Other Organizations	54
IV.	Local Field Excursions by Moseley's Classes from the Sandusky High School, 1891-1903, by Various Writers and Editors	55
V.	The High School Museum at Sandusky	57
VI.	List of Writings in Manuscript about Moseley by Ronald L. Stuckey	61

BIOGRAPHICAL SOURCES

I.	Sketches, Commentaries, Stories	63
II.	Obituaries	68
III.	Will and Estate	69

GUIDE TO ARCHIVES

I.	Archives for the book, *Edwin Lincoln Moseley (1865-1948), Naturalist, Scientist, Educator* (1998)	71
II.	Biographical Sources of Individuals in the Archives for the book, *Edwin Lincoln Moseley* (1998)	76

A BIOGRAPHICAL SKETCH BY IVAN E. LAKE 79
MOSELEY'S ADMIRERS SADDENED BY HIS DEATH;
PRAISED AS A GENIUS AND HUMANITARIAN [6 JUNE 1948] 84
PHOTOGRAPHIC ILLUSTRATIONS 0,11,15,29,33,42,46,62,70,78,83
TITLE PAGES OF MOSELEY'S PUBLICATIONS x,2,6,12,16,18,24,30,34

OTHER WORLDS

BY
EDWIN LINCOLN MOSELEY, A.M.
HEAD OF THE DEPARTMENT OF BIOLOGY
OHIO STATE NORMAL COLLEGE

D. APPLETON AND COMPANY
NEW YORK :: 1933 :: LONDON

Title page from Moseley's book, *Other Worlds* (1933).

SCIENTIFIC CONTRIBUTIONS

I. Contributions to Astronomy   Archive No. 1060
(Meteors and other Worlds)

1903.   The meteor of September 15, 1902. (Abstract). *Eleventh Annual Report Ohio State Academy of Science* 1902: 26. **ELM**.

1904.   Meteor of September 15, 1902. *Popular Astronomy* 12:190-192. (Also, *Sandusky Register*, 19 March, p. 9). **ELM**.

1909.   "Prof. Moseley will search skies for Halley's Comet." *Sandusky Register*, 1 December, p. 4.

1919.   "Moseley to tell of meteors here . . ." *Sandusky Star-Journal*, 22 April, p. 12. **ELM**.

1919.   "Where do meteors come from?" *Sandusky Register*, 25 April, p. 11. **ELM**.

1919.   "Meteorites will be shown Sunday. Prof. Moseley gives some interesting facts regarding stones from heavens." *Sandusky Star-Journal*, 26 April, p. 9. **ELM**.

1919.   "Star showers." *Sandusky Register*, 28 May, p. 7. **ELM**.

1926.   "Prof. Moseley discusses meteors and meteorites." *Sandusky Register*, 25 March, p. 5.

1931.   Are there creatures like ourselves in other worlds? *Scientific American* 145(5): 308-310. (Also, *Sandusky Register*, 22 November, p. 12; revised as chapter XIX, In *Other Worlds*, pp. 215-226. 1933). **ELM**. (Review, *Bee Gee News* 16 (10):1. 24 November 1931).

*1933.   *Other Worlds*. D. Appleton and Co., New York. xi, 231 pp. **ELM**. (Reviews, *Sandusky Star-Journal*, 12 December 1932, p. 5; *Bee Gee News* 17(9):1. 9 November 1932; *Bee Gee News* 17(31): 1. 3 May 1933).

1

Ohio State Academy of Science.

SPECIAL PAPERS NO. 1.

SANDUSKY FLORA.

A CATALOGUE

OF THE

FLOWERING PLANTS and FERNS

GROWING WITHOUT CULTIVATION, IN ERIE COUNTY, OHIO, AND THE PENINSULA AND ISLANDS OF OTTAWA COUNTY,

By E. L. MOSELEY, A. M.

PUBLISHED BY THE ACADEMY OF SCIENCE,
MAY, 1899.

PRESS OF CLAPPER PRINTING CO.
WOOSTER, OHIO.

Title page from Moseley's paper, "Sandusky Flora" (1899).

II. Contributions to Botany   Archive No. 1061
(Floras of Sandusky area and Oak Openings in Lucas County)

1892. "To stimulate botanical study [by giving prizes to students adding to the list of 448 species of local plants]." *Sandusky Sunday Register*, 17 April, p. 1.

1894. "Attractions for a scientist [in the vicinity of Sandusky]. Prof. Moseley's masterly paper before The [Ohio] Academy of Science." *Sandusky Register*, 30 December 1894, p. 5; *Sandusky Weekly Register*, 2 January 1895, p. 10.

1895. Attractions for a scientist in the vicinity of Sandusky. (Abstract). *Third Annual Report Ohio State Academy of Science* 1895: 5. **ELM**.

1896. A comparison of the flora of Erie Co., Ohio, with that of Erie Co., N.Y. (Abstract). *Science*, new series 4: 434; *Botanical Gazette* 22: 224. **ELM**.

1896. "The plants and flowers of Erie County." *Sandusky Register*, 15 April, p. 5; *Sandusky Weekly Register*, 22 April, p. 5. **ELM**.

1897. Climatic influence of Lake Erie on vegetation. *American Naturalist* 31: 60-63. **ELM**. (Review notice by Charles E. Bessey. *American Naturalist* 31: 62-63).

1897. "A comparison of the flora about the east end of Lake Erie with that of the Islands, Peninsulas and neighboring mainland near the west end." *Sandusky Weekly Journal*, 6 February, p. 4. **ELM**. (Notice of this article printed in *Sandusky Register*, 2 February 1897, p. 8).

1897. "[The] Ohio State University. Valuable additions [by E. L. Moseley] to the Botanical and Geological Departments." *Sandusky Register*, 11 February, p. 5. L. R. Martell.

1898. Reversion of loments to leaves in ticktrefoil. *Sixth Annual Report Ohio State Academy of Science* 1897: 32 + discussion 32-34. **ELM**.

1899. Sandusky Flora. *The Lakeside Magazine* 5(3): 7-13. **ELM**.

*1899. Sandusky Flora. A catalogue of the flowering plants and ferns growing without cultivation, in Erie County, Ohio, and the peninsula and islands of Ottawa County. *Ohio State Academy of Science, Special Papers*, No. 1. 167 pp. **ELM**. (Review by J. C. Arthur. *Botanical Gazette* 28: 139-140. 1899).

1903. Additions and corrections to the Sandusky flora. (Abstract). *Eleventh Annual Report Ohio State Academy of Science* 1902: 27. **ELM**.

1905. "Our Museum [Herbarium]," p. 10. *In Sandusky Register*, 16 June, pp. 9-10. Carroll C. Page.

1908. *Solidago moseleyi*, p. 93. *In* Notes on some plants of northeastern America. *Rhodora* 10: 46-55,84-95. Merritt L. Fernald.

1911. "Interesting exhibits at our high school museum. Many visitors were astounded to find display occupies seven rooms—Prof. Moseley comments on economic botany specimens [basswood]." *Sandusky Register*, 10 March, p. 4. **ELM**.

1912. *Thalictrum moseleyi*, pp. 294,295. *In* Western meadow rues—1. *American Midland Naturalist* 2: 290-296. Edward L. Greene.

1923. "Moseley has *Cypress* specimens thought to be 20,000 years old [from Washington, D. C.]." *Sandusky Star-Journal*, 3 September, p. 2.

1923. "Moseley gets big puff ball [from near Monclova, Lucas County]." *Sandusky Register*, 27 September, p. 8.

1924. "Prof. Moseley discovers rare orchid specimen [*Spiranthes gracilis*] on [Marblehead] Peninsula." *Sandusky Star-Journal*, 1 October, p. 3. (Letter to the *Star-Journal*). **ELM**.

1925. "Strange sedge in trout stream [at Castalia, Ohio. *Carex aurea*. *C. teretiuscula*]." *Sandusky Register*, 5 July, Section 2, p. 1. **ELM**.

1926. "Finds new plant [*Rhamnus lanceolata*] in Ottawa County." *Daily Advertiser*, Tiffin, Ohio, 1 June, p. 2.

1926. "Prof. Moseley gives lecture last evening [on 'The flora of Sandusky and vicinity and wild flower preservation']." *Sandusky Register*, 8 May, p. 2. [Summary].

1926. "[Moseley discovers phosphorescent mushroom near Bowling Green]." *Sandusky Register*, 24 August, p. 10.

1927. "Moseley finds rare poison hemlock plant [at Grand Rapids, Ohio], . . . Provided death potion for Greek Socrates." *Sandusky Register*, 1 September, p. 2.

*1928. Flora of the Oak Openings west of Toledo. *Proceedings of the Ohio Academy of Science* 8: 79-134. S*pecial Paper* No. 20. **ELM**. (Commentary by Jeanne Hawkins. *Toledo Naturalist's Association Yearbook* 24:45-48. 1968).

1930. "Botany students enjoy trip to Catawba Island." *Bee Gee News* 14(8): 3. 23 May.

1931. Some plants that were probably brought to northern Ohio from the West by Indians. *Papers of the Michigan Academy Science, Arts and Letters* (1930) 13: 169-172. (Also, *Sandusky Register*, 15 March, p. 10). **ELM**.

1931. "Dried specimens of lotus plant [*Nelumbo lutea*] to be shown at museum Sunday."*Sandusky Register*, 18 April, p. 2. **ELM**.

1931. "Prof. Moseley to show mushrooms: will exhibit fungi growths at high school museum." *Sandusky Star-Journal*, 3 December, p. 2. **[ELM]**.

1934. "Field trip to the Oak Openings [to observe vegetation, under the direction of E. L. Moseley]." *Bee Gee News* 23(39): 1. 5 July 1934.

1938. What may be learned from stumps? *School Science and Mathematics* 38:528-533. **ELM**.

1947. "Oak Openings oasis." *Toledo Naturalist's Association Bulletin* 1(9):3. **ELM**.

1984. Some rare and infrequent flora of the Oak Openings: Addenda to Professor Moseley's findings. *Northwestern Ohio Quarterly* 56(1): 18-20. Winter. Nathan William Easterly.

1995. Erie Sand Barrens State Nature Preserve [a Moseley plant-study site in Erie County, Ohio]. *Newsletter, Division of Natural Areas and Preserves* 17(4): 1-2. October, November, December. [Guy L. Denny, ed.].

1997. Edwin Lincoln Moseley's botany class field trips. *Ohio Journal of Science* 97(2): A-24. [Abstract]. Relda E. Niederhofer.

LAKE ERIE

Floods Lake Levels
Northeast Storms

The Formation of Sandusky Bay and
Cedar Point

by
Edwin Lincoln Moseley

A Reprint by

The Ohio Historical Society
Columbus, Ohio
1973

**Title page from Moseley's reprinted paper on
"The Formation of Sandusky Bay and Cedar Point" (1973).**

III. Contributions to Geology Archive No. 1062
(Submerged Valleys and Underground Rivers)

1894. "Attractions for a scientist [in the vicinity of Sandusky]. Prof. Moseley's masterly paper before The [Ohio] Academy of Science." *Sandusky Register*, 30 December 1894, p. 5; *Sandusky Weekly Register*, 2 January 1895, p. 10.

1895. Attractions for a scientist in the vicinity of Sandusky. (Abstract). *Third Annual Report Ohio State Academy of Science* 1895: 5. **ELM**.

1898. "[Moseley and students explore caves at Put-in-Bay]." *Sandusky Register*, 12 March, p. 5; *Sandusky Weekly Register*, 16 March, p. 4. Theresa Thorndale.

*1898. Lake Erie enlarging. The Islands separated from the mainland in recent times. *The Lakeside Magazine* 1(9): 14-20. **ELM**.

1901. "Heights and distances in Sandusky." *Sandusky Star-Journal*, 14 December, p. 20. **ELM**.

1902. Submerged valleys in Sandusky Bay. *National Geographic Magazine* 13: 398-403. **ELM**.

1902. "Lake currents. Professor Moseley is endeavoring to ascertain their direction." *Sandusly Register*, 3 August, p. 8; *Sandusky Weekly Register*, 6 August, p. 12.

1902. "Sandusky to be under a deluge in coming years. Prof. Moseley and other geologists find evidence that lakes are encroaching on land in the east." *Sandusky Daily Star*, 19 November, p. 3.

1902. "Paper by E. L. Moseley. Currents of Sandusky Bay topic before Academy of Science." *Sandusky Register*, 29 November, p. 3. (Contains titles and authors of papers to be presented).

1902. "Currents in Sandusky Bay are not persistent—Prof. Moseley's findings." *Sandusky Star-Journal*, 1 December, p. 6.

1902. "Original work of Prof. Moseley in high school explained to scientists." *Sandusky Daily Star*, 4 June, p. 3.

1902. "Wonders of Put-in-Bay subterranean caves. High School students and alumni to study them—an interesting excursion." *Sandusky Daily Star*, 22 May, p. 3.

1902. "How the currents act in the Bay of Sandusky. Travelling bottles brought information to E. L. Moseley which he gave before the Ohio State Academy of Science." *Sandusky Register*, 3 December 1902, p. 5; *Sandusky Weekly Register*, 3 December 1902, p. 3.

1902. "[Mapping the channels of Sandusky Bay] Original work for the high school teacher. A paper by Prof. E. L. Moseley, read at an Ann Arbor (Mich.) Teachers' Meeting, last spring." *Sandusky Daily Star*, 20 December, p. 5. **ELM**.

1903. [Evidence for the westward expansion of Lake Erie] Original work in high schools. *Ohio Educational Monthly* 52: 367-374. **ELM**.

1903. The currents in Sandusky Bay. *Eleventh Annual Report Ohio State Academy of Science* 1902: 21-26. **ELM**. (Notice of this article printed in *Sandusky Register*, 29 November 1902, p. 3; *Sandusky Star-Journal*, 1 December 1902, p. 6).

1903. Testing the currents in Lake Erie. *National Geographic Magazine* 14: 41-42. **ELM**.

1903. Currents in Sandusky Bay. *Monthly Weather Review* 31: 236. **ELM**.

1903. "Another bottle [appears], after its long Lake [Erie] journey." *Sandusky Register*, 11 June, p. 2.

1903. "The current in Sandusky Bay." *Sandusky Register*, 8 June, p. 2; *Sandusky Weekly Register*, 17 June, p. 8. **ELM**.

1903. Rainfall and the level of Lake Erie. *National Geographic Magazine* 14: 327-328. **ELM**. (Notice of this article published in *Sandusky Evening Star*, 19 August, p. 3).

1903. " Tilting of earth will keep Lake levels up. Prof. E. L. Moseley shows relation between rainfall and levels and why there is no fear of lower water." *Sandusky Evening Star*, 19 August, p. 3. **ELM**.

1904. "Searching for river bed [in Sandusky Bay]." *Seneca Advertiser*, Tiffin, Ohio, 7 January, p. 8.

1904. "Evidence of better ground for an east end channel [in Sandusky Bay]. Discovery has been made of a route in which there is much less rock, and which will give access to fine dock facilities." *Sandusky Star-Journal*, 11 February, p. 6.

1904. "[Determining the flow of underground water from Bellevue]." *Seneca Advertiser*, Tiffin, Ohio, 31 March, p. 3; *Erie County Reporter*, 7 April, p. 1.

1904. "Sink holes near Bellevue." *Seneca Advertiser*, Tiffin, Ohio, 14 April, p. 7.

1904. "[Excursion to Put-in-Bay to visit caves]." *The Fram* [Sandusky High School], 3(7): 15. May.

1904. "President Moseley of Sandusky . . . told of the formation of Sandusky Bay and Cedar Point." *Sandusky Weekly Register*, 30 November, p. 4.

*1905. Formation of Sandusky Bay and Cedar Point. *Thirteenth Annual Report Ohio State Academy of Science* 1904: 179-238; *Proceedings of the Ohio Academy of Science* 4: 179-238. (Reprinted under the title *Lake Erie: Floods, Lake Levels, Northeast Storms. The Formation of Sandusky Bay and Cedar Point*. The Ohio Historical Society, Columbus. ii, 64 pp. 1973). **ELM**.

1905. Change of level at the west end of Lake Erie. (Abstract). *Seventh Annual Report Michigan Academy of Science* 1905: 38-39. **ELM**.

1906. "Sandusky Bay and Cedar Point: Their formation—the changes wrought by the hand of time. What the waters have covered in ages past—nature's silent forces." *Sandusky Register*, 20 January, pp. 9-12; *Sandusky Weekly Register*, 24 January, pp. 13-16. **ELM**.

1909. "Ancient rock valley [from Willard to east of Huron]." *Erie County Reporter*, 22 July, p. 4. (Reprinted under the title "Moseley discovers ancient valley," *In* Charles E. Frohman. *Sandusky Area Miscellany*, Item 54. The Ohio Historical Society. [Columbus]. 1973).

1909. [Excerpts from Moseley's 1904 address to The Ohio Academy of Science on the "Formation of Sandusky Bay and Cedar Point]," p. 49. *In* Twentieth Century History of Sandusky County, Ohio. Richmond-Arnold Co., Chicago. 934 pp. Basil Meek.

1913. "Outlet of Bellevue's mysterious underground river sought in vain. Prof. E. L. Moseley, . . . among those who have studied the case—The Castalia Blue Hole." *Sandusky Register*, 9 April, p. 1.

1914. "Points of interest around Sandusky, and interesting bits of their history." *Sandusky Register*, 13 June, p. 7. (Reprinted under the title "A trip with Professor Moseley." *In* Charles E. Frohman. *Sandusky Area Miscellany*, Item 100. The Ohio Historical Society. [Columbus]. 1973). **ELM**.

1917. "[Depths of Sandusky Bay to help shipbuilding plant project]." *Sandusky Register*, 16 March, p. 12.

1920. "Water deepening in lakes; Ohio scientist tells why." *Sandusky Star-Journal*, 17 July, p. 8.

1921. "How Professor Moseley helped locate Huron Railroad Bridge by finding pre-glacial valley." *Sandusky Star-Journal*, 7 May, Section 2, p. 9. (Excerpt reprinted under the title, "Moseley and the Huron River Bridge." *In* Charles E. Frohman, *Sandusky Area Miscellany*, Item 22. The Ohio Historical Society, [Columbus]. 1973).

1922. "Nature played big part in making Sandusky one of the garden spots of the world." *Sandusky Register*, 31 December, pp. 4, 14. **ELM**.

1923. "Moseley investigates geological formation [pre-glacial valley from Huron to Norwalk]." *Sandusky Register*, 3 August, p.10.

1925. "Blue Hole said to be 43 feet deep." *Huron County Reporter*, 6 August, p. 1.

1929. "Why Lake Erie is higher." *Sandusky Star-Journal*, 13 September, p. 5. **ELM**.

1937. "Reasons for Bellevue flood explained by Prof. Moseley. Scientist says land has sunk, leaving holes that had no surface outlets to drain water from torrential rains." *Toledo Blade*, 13 July, p. 16; *Sandusky Register*, 18 July, p. 3.

1959. "Channel finally named for Dr. Moseley. Early Sandusky teacher charted muddy [Sandusky] Bay bottom."*Sandusky Register*, 21 December, p. 7.

1960. "Sandusky outer channel named for Moseley." *Bowling Green State University Magazine* 1:22. February.

1973. "Geologist [Moseley] predicted Erie flooding in 1904. Port Clinton under water by 2050?" *Sandusky Register*, 16 February, pp. 15-16. Abner John Katzman.

1973. "Lake levels didn't stump him [Moseley], trees clue to heavy rains." [Name of newspaper not known]. Rochester, New York, 20 May, p. 4.

1974. "Sandusky Bay Channels." "Learning with Professor Moseley [Comparing the size of Sandusky Bay with the ocean]." *In* Charles E. Frohman, *Sandusky Potpourri*, Items 10 and 42. The Ohio Historical Society, [Columbus]. 1974).

SCIENTIFIC CONTRIBUTIONS/GEOLOGY — ARCHIVE No. 1062

Dr. Stuckey's book, *Edwin Lincoln Moseley (1865-1948): Naturalist, Scientist, Educator* was published in December, 1998 and is co-authored with his former student, Mrs. Relda E. Niederhofer of Sandusky.

The 320-page hard bound book with 85 illustrations concerns the frugal lifestyle and the significant scientific contributions of Professor Moseley who was a distinguished naturalist and educator in the Sandusky High School (1899-1914) and the first Professor of Science in the newly-founded Bowling Green Normal College (1914-1936). He continued there as an emeritus professor and curator of the Museum until his death in 1948.

The authors present Moseley's life and scientific achievements in an informative style in 12 of the 20 chapters. Other chapters are developed out of notes and writings of those who knew him - college presidents, former students, and natural science writers. Two chapters are of Moseley's own unpublished writings - a selection of letters and Sandusky's scientific and economic advantages.

Among Moseley's accomplishments discussed in the book are his recognition for the discovery of the cause of milk sickness, his thorough studies of the plants of the Sandusky area and the Oak Openings west of Toledo, his mapping of the pre-glacial river channels in Sandusky Bay and Erie County, his accurate long-range weather forecasts which predicted the high water levels of Lake Erie in the 1970's, and his innovative teaching methods. He was widely known for taking students into the field to study the plants and animals in their natural habitats, long before it became a more common practice in schools and colleges. According to Charles E. Herdendorf, former director of the Ohio State University's F.T. Stone Laboratory at Put-in-Bay, "Moseley's legacy lives on in the spirit of instruction at the .... Laboratory, Ohio's biological field station on Lake Erie for over one hundred years."

In the Preface, Stuckey recalls that his mother Leora Shuey, a one-room school teacher in Eden Township, Seneca County, and who attended Bowling Green Normal College, spoke often of Moseley and clipped items about him from the Tiffin *Advertiser-Tribune*. In 1966, when Stuckey first began teaching at the F.T. Stone Laboratory, he also began his long-term botanical studies on the changes in the flora of Lake Erie and its associated wetlands. For these studies he needed to review Moseley's work on the subject, and thus began his investigation into his life and contributions.

Stuckey Speaks About Moseley Book.

(Taken 25 April 1999 by Linda Hengst for RLS)

11

MEAT, SUGAR, WHITE FLOUR DIET INADEQUATE, SAYS DR. MOSELEY

Dr. E. L. Moseley, professor emeritus of Bowling Green State University, writes anent the meat shortage.

Editor, Sentinel – Tribune.

Many people living in Bowling Green think they are fortunate because they are not threatened with a shortage of meat. Probably they have been eating more meat than is good for them.

In the United States, a large part of the food consumed consists of meat, along with a score of different articles made of white flour and a dozen or more that contain a good deal of white sugar. None of these three things is harmful when used in small amount, but to depend upon them to supply the greater part of our nourishment is unwise. Such a diet fails to afford an adequate amount of minerals, vitamins, and amino acids. All of these may be obtained by using a greater variety of foods.

Since no one particular kind of food is indispensable, it should be possible for any person to obtain a good variety without undue expense. The cost can be reduced by raising some of them in a garden. The improved health, comfort, efficiency and longer life resulting from a better choice of foods will more than offset any additional cost. Improvement of the diet should enable many persons to dispense with medicine and also with frequent visits to a doctor's office.

There are hundreds of kinds of good foods. It is a pity that anyone should suppose that those with which one is unfamiliar are not worth trying. Prejudices against some kinds may be due to the poor quality, immaturity, or improper preparation given them the first time they were eaten.

Some benefit would probably result from a more frequent use of any of the following:- brown bread of good quality, whether made of wheat or rye oatmeal, various kinds of dark colored breakfast foods; corn meal and sweet corn; peas; different kinds of beans, including soy beans; carrots; cabbage and related vegetables; asparagus; potatoes; yams; greens of any kind that appeal to the appetite; more than thirty kinds of fruit, including fresh, dry, and canned fruit.

Eating in a hurry or when one has more need for rest than for food may be worse than eating food that has not been well prepared for the table. E. L. Moseley.

Essay on diet by Moseley reprinted from the *Daily Sentinel-Tribune*, Bowling Green, Ohio (1946).

IV. Contributions to Health & Hygiene   Archive No. 1063
(Diet, Cooking of Foods, and Extermination of Mosquitoes)

1892.   "What we eat. Prof. Moseley gives an interesting lecture on foods." *Sandusky Register*, 15 February, p. 4; *Sandusky Weekly Register*, 17 February, p. 5.

1893.   "Prof. Moseley gave the first of a series of talks on *Sanitary Science* on Monday." *Sandusky Register,* 15 December, p. 2.

1900.   "Prof. Moseley gives a short talk on sanitary science at the high school. Notice." *Sandusky Register*, 1 December, p. 2. Jessie Horning, ed.

1902.   "[Value of a teacher's health. Original work for the high school teacher. A paper by Prof. E. L. Moseley, read at an Ann Arbor (Mich.) Teachers' Meeting last spring." *Sandusky Daily Star*, 20 December, p. 5. **ELM**.

1903.   "Prof. Moseley tells how to exterminate the mosquito." *Sandusky Star-Journal*, 10 June, p. 6; *Sandusky Weekly Star*, 11 June 1903, p. 5.

1903.   "Talked on mosquitoes. Mr. Moseley says if none were here, values would rise." *Sandusky Register*, 11 June, p. 2.

1903.   "Malaria and mosquitoes. Hints by Prof. Moseley of the high school." *Sandusky Register*, 19 June, p. 2. **ELM**.

1904.   "Stuart Hamilton. Prof. Moseley writes of his condition [of appendicitis] and rough experience on freight trains with tramps." *Sandusky Register*, 11 July, p. 5. **ELM**.

1910.   Aluminum cooking vessels questioned. *The Ohio Farmer* 126: 622. 31 December. Reply by **ELM**.

1911.   "Says danger lurks in the aluminum cooking utensils. Prof. E. L. Moseley announces results of interesting research through farmers' paper." *Sandusky Register*, 8 January, p. 8.

1911.   Action of acids and soda on aluminum. *The Ohio Farmer* 127: 61. 14 January. (Commentary on Moseley's article in *The Ohio Farmer*, 31 December 1910, by Harriet Mason).

1911. Effect of foods on aluminum. *The Ohio Farmer* 127: 164-167. 4 February. (Commentary by editor and articles by E. Blough, **E. L. Moseley**, and Maude Meredith).

1911. "Experiments with organic acids and aluminum-wares. Head of Department of Science of Sandusky High School announces valuable discoveries in current issue of *The Ohio Farmer*." *Sandusky Register*, 22 February, p. 4.

1911. Housekeepers' interest in gill-netted fish. *The Ohio Farmer* 127: 630-631. 20 May. (Also, *Sandusky Register*, 30 May 1914, p. 4). **ELM**.

1912. Disease germs in and out of the body. *The Ohio Farmer* 129: 690-691. 1 June. **ELM**.

1912. "Prof. Moseley writes interesting treatise on disease germs." *Sandusky Register*, 7 December, p. 5. **ELM**.

1912. Some ways of teaching pupils practical hygiene. *School Science and Mathematics* 12: 1-5. **ELM**.

1913. "Deadly disease germs will be shown at high school museum. Prof. Moseley announces exhibitions of unusual interest to the public, ..." *Sandusky Register*, 11 April, p. 5.

1925. "The use of poisons." *Bee Gee News* 6(4):10. January 28. **ELM**.

1929. "In 50 years, E. L. Moseley hasn't missed day from class through illness." *Sandusky Register*, 21 July 1929, p. 5.

1936. "Bowling Green Professor hasn't missed class in 50 years because of illness. Took time out for journeys to far places." *Toledo Sunday Times*, 10 May, p. 9.

1946. "Meat, sugar, white flour diet inadequate, says Dr. Moseley." *Daily Sentinel-Tribune*, Bowling Green, 24 January, p. 4. **ELM**.

1946. "Diet, droughts keep retired Bee Gee scientist happy as long-range predictions materialize. Dr. Moseley at 81 continues study of tree rings." *Toledo Sunday Times*, 20 October, p. 23; (Based on News Release, B.G.S.U., 19 October 1946. Typewritten, 3 pp.). Paul W. Jones. [Not located in the newspaper].

1946. "Drouths, proper diet keep B.G.S.U. educator healthy." *Columbus Dispatch*, 27 October, p. 2A.

SCIENTIFIC CONTRIBUTIONS/HEALTH & HYGIENE   ARCHIVE No. 1063

Moseley Hall

Students near Moseley Hall on Bowling Green State University campus.

(Taken 4 April 1997 by Ronald L. Stuckey)

MILK SICKNESS CAUSED BY WHITE SNAKEROOT

By
EDWIN LINCOLN MOSELEY

Professor Emeritus of Biology
State University, Bowling Green, Ohio
Past-President of Ohio Academy of Science

Published jointly by
The Ohio Academy of Science
and
The Author

Presented to Hazel Stockdale by the author, Edwin Lincoln Moseley.

BOWLING GREEN, OHIO
1941

Author's signature in Hazel Stockdale's copy of Moseley's book.

(Gift from her nephew Thomas M. Stockdale; Stuckey Collection)

V. Contributions to Medical Science   Archive No. 1064
(Milk Sickness)

1905.   "Specimens of tremble weed secured by Prof. Moseley. White snake root alleged to have caused milk sickness, found in locality where the disease appeared." *Sandusky Star-Journal*, 1 November, p. 6.

1906.   "Says tremble-weed is cause of milk-sickness. Prof. Moseley is prepared to prove claim at anytime." *Sandusky Register*. 25 January, p. 8.

*1906.   The cause of trembles in cattle, sheep and horses and of milk-sickness in people. *Ohio Naturalist* 6: 463-470, 477-483. (Also, *Sandusky Register*, 28 April, pp. 9, 11; *Sandusky Weekly Register*, 9 May, p. 10). **ELM**.

1909.   The cause of trembles and milk sickness. *The Medical Record* 75: 839-844. (Reprinted, William Wood & Co., pp. 1-20). **ELM**.

1909.   "Dreaded sickness traced to the white snake root." *Toledo Daily Blade*, 3 December, p. 13; "To exterminate white snake root as a result of Prof. Moseley's discovery of the cause of milk sickness . . . ." *Sandusky Register*, 4 December, p. 6.

1909.   "[On the cause of trembles and milk sickness]." *Mulford's Veterinary Bulletin*, Philadelphia. [Efforts to locate this item have failed]. **ELM**.

1910.   Antidote for aluminum phosphate, the poison that causes milk sickness. *The Medical Record* 77: 620-622. (Reprinted, William Wood & Co., pp. 1-6). **ELM**.

1910.   White snakeroot. The cause of trembles and milk sickness. *The Ohio Farmer* 126: 320. 15 October. (Also, *Sandusky Register*, 15 October, p. 5; *Sandusky Weekly Register*, 19 October, p. 2). **ELM**.

1910.   Milk sickness—trembles. *The Ohio Farmer* 126: 476. 26 November. **ELM**.

1917.   Milk sickness and trembles caused by resin of white snakeroot. *The Medical Record* 92: 428. (Notice of this article published in the *Sandusky Register*, 10 October, p. 10). **ELM**.

1919.   The connection of milksickness with the poisonous qualities of white snakeroot (*Eupatorium urticaefolium*). *Journal of Infectious Diseases* 24: 231-259. Walter G. Sackett. [Credit given to Moseley, pp. 236-238].

(Continued on page 19, bottom)

90-YEAR FORECAST ON WEATHER MADE

Dr. Moseley's Predictions Are Based on Tree-Ring Widths and Lake-Level Records

RAINFALL CYCLE TESTED

Michigan Scientists Assured of 'Considerable Probability' In Biologist's Prophecies

Title given to Moseley's paper on "90-Year Weather Forcast" in *The New York Times* (1939).

VI. Contributions to Meteorology   Archive No. 1065
(Tree Stumps, Rainfall, Droughts, and Floods)

1897.   Climatic influence of Lake Erie on vegetation. *American Naturalist* 31: 60-63. **ELM**. (Review notice by Charles E. Bessey. *American Naturalist* 31: 62-63).

1897.   "A comparison of the [climate and] flora about the east end of Lake Erie with that of the Islands, Peninsula and neighboring mainland near the west end." *Sandusky Weekly Register*, 6 February, p. 4. **ELM**.

1903.   Rainfall and the level of Lake Erie. *National Geographic Magazine* 14: 327-328. **ELM**. (Notice of this article published in *Sandusky Evening Star*, 19 August, p. 3).

1903.   "Tilting of earth will keep Lake levels up. Prof. E. L. Moseley shows relation between rainfall and levels and why there is no fear of lower water." *Sandusky Evening Star,* 19 August, p. 3.

1908.   "The remarkable fog of last Sunday night. Local scientist tells how the smoke induced a London Fog in Sandusky." *Sandusky Register,* 19 September, p. 5. **ELM**.

1929.   "Why Lake Erie is higher." *Sandusky Star-Journal,* 13 September, p. 5. **ELM**.

1937.   "Prof. Moseley predicts forty-six years wet weather ahead." *Daily Sentinel-Tribune*, Bowling Green, 31 March, pp. 1, 2. [**ELM**; Ivan E. Lake]. (Moseley's first rainfall prediction; given at banquet in his honor upon retirement from teaching, Bowling Green State University, 30 March, 1937).

Contributions to Medical Science (Continued from page 17)

1927.   Beware of milk sickness. Poison lurks in Ohio woodland pastures. *The Ohio Farmer* 160(11):9, 25. 10 September. Albert A. Hansen. [Credits Moseley with the discovery that trembles in cattle is caused by their grazing on the plant white snakeroot, which in turn causes milk sickness in human beings].

*1941.   *Milk sickness caused by white snakeroot*. Ohio Academy of Science and the author. Special Papers No. 22. 171 pp. **ELM**. (Review notice by G. W. B[laydes]. *Ohio Journal of Science* 43: 266. 1943; Prof. Moseley's latest book, "Milk Sickness," wins praise, [from an unidentified newspaper clipping, Bowling Green State University Library]).

1937. "Who says 'It ain't gonna rain no more?' Prof. Moseley, after research, sees 46-year wet weather cycle ahead." *Sandusky Star-Journal,* 3 April, pp. 1, 3. **[ELM]**. (Moseley's first rainfall prediction; given at banquet in his honor upon retirement from teaching, Bowling Green State University, 30 March, 1937).

1937. "Moseley writes on vagaries of weather." *Bee Gee News* 21(38): 1, 4. 30 June. **[ELM]**.

1938. "Heavy rains to continue, expert says. New 45-year cycle of wet weather said to have started in 1936." *Toledo Blade,* 11 April, p. 12.

1938. "Professor Moseley sees Sandusky area in midst of [wet] rainfall cycle." *Sandusky Register,* 2 June, pp. 1, 3. (Letter to the *Register*). **ELM**.

*1938. What may be learned from stumps? *School Science and Mathematics* 38: 528-533. **ELM**.

1939. "Scientist says tree rings foretell rain by 90 years." *Detroit News,* 18 March, p. —. Allen Shoenfield. [Page number not verified].

1939. "90-year forecast on weather made. Dr. Moseley's predictions are based on tree-ring widths and lake-level records. Rainfall cycle tested. Michigan scientists assured of considerable probability in biologist's prophecies." *New York Times,* 19 March, Section III-p. 4.

1939. "Weather, past and to come." *New York Times,* 10 August, p. 18.

1939. "Sees much rain from May to August, 1940; Professor Moseley, former Sanduskian, has prediction." *Sandusky Star-Journal,* 9 October, pp. 1, 6. (Based on News Release, B.G.S.U., October 1939. Typewritten, 2 pp., Duncan Scott).

*1939. Long time forecasts of Ohio River floods. *Ohio Journal of Science* 39: 220-231. **ELM**. (*Biological Abstracts* 14: 567. 1940).

1939. The dating tree rings. *Toledo Naturalists Association, Annual Bulletin.* 1939 (7):30-32. **ELM**.

*1940. The ninety-nine year precipitation cycle. *Papers of the Michigan Academy of Science, Arts, and Letters* (1939) 25: 491-496. **ELM**. (*Biological Abstracts* 14: 1105-1106).

1940. "Weather Predictions [of Professor E. L. Moseley]." News Release, B.G.S.U., May 1940. Typewritten, 1 p. Duncan Scott.

*1941. Sun-spots and tree rings. *Journal of the Royal Astronomical Society of Canada* 35:376-392. **ELM**.

1942. "[Summer's excessive rain proves accuracy of Moseley's predictions]." News Release, B.G.S.U., 22 August 1942. Typewritten, 1 p. 40 copies mailed. Paul W. Jones.

1942. "Publication has article by former local resident [E. L. Moseley] concerning precipitation." *Sandusky Register*, 14 December, p. 3. (Based on News Release, B.G.S.U., 10 December 1942. Typewritten. 2 pp. 3 copies mailed). [Paul W. Jones].

1942. Solar influence on variations in rainfall in the interior of the United States. *Popular Astronomy* 50:419-422. **ELM**. (Reprinted, 3 pp.; notice of article printed in *Sandusky Register*, 14 December, p. 3).

1943. "Moseley predicted Grand Finale of rain this spring." *Sandusky Register*, 20 May, p. 1. (Based on News Release, B.G.S.U., 20 May 1943. Typewritten 1 p. 90 copies mailed). Paul W. Jones.

1943. "[He 'calls' floods and drouths years-centuries ahead]. News Release, B.G.S.U., 10 July 1943. Typewritten, 6 pp. Paul W. Jones. (Sent to *Cleveland Plain Dealer*, but not located in the newspaper).

1943. "Prof. Moseley says south shore of Lake Erie will have high water again in 1946." *Sandusky Register*, 10 August, p. 1. (Based on News Release, B.G.S.U., 7 August 1943. Typewritten 5 pp.) Paul W. Jones. (Contains Moseley's prediction of water levels in Lake Erie, from 1944 to 1976).

1943. Long-range weather man: [E. L. Moseley], an Ohio scientist, with a remarkable record of accuracy, gives C. G. readers a forecast of dry and wet periods in years ahead. *Country Gentleman* 113(1): 12, 38, 40, November. Moran Tudury.

1944. "Dr. Moseley has forecast on precipitation outlook." *Sandusky Register Star-News*, 13 July, pp. 1, 8. (Based on News Release, B.G.S.U., [13 July 1944]. Typewritten, 2 pp.). Ken H. McFall.

1944. Precipitation prospects, 1943-47, for Ohio and near-by states. *Papers of the Michigan Academy of Sciences, Arts and Letters* (1943) 29: 23-29. **ELM**. (Notice of this article published in *Sandusky Register Star-News,* 15 July, pp. 1,8).

1944. Recurrence of floods and droughts after intervals of about 90.4 years. *Popular Astronomy* 52: 284-287. **ELM**.

1945. Tree stumps as weather indicators. *American Fruit Grower* 65: 36-37. **ELM**.

1945. "[Moseley predicts rainfall much above average in late 1945 and early part of 1946]." News Release, B.G.S.U., 1945, Typewritten, 2 pp. Ken H. McFall.

1945. "Ohio seer visions drought in 1947. Noted Bowling Green scientist studies tree rings." *Sandusky Register*, 26 August, p. 1. Zenith Henkin.

1945. "Tree rings indicate 1947 will bring midwest drought." *Buffalo Evening News*, 8 September, p. —. Zenith Henkin. [Page number not verified].

1945. "Prophet of rain sees little of it next year." *Chicago Daily News*, 19 September, p. 20. Gene Morgan.

1945. "Weather or not—wet or dry, hot or cold, Toledo's climate offers whatever you want—or don't want." *Toledo Times*, 30 October, p. _. Don Wolfe. [Not located in the newspaper].

1946. "[Drought in 1946 and 1947, predicted in 1939, to begin Soon]." News Release, B.G.S.U., 30 April 1946. Typewritten, 2 pp.

1946. "[Drought soon to begin in 1946 and 1947]." News Release, B.G.S.U., 14 May. Typewritten 4 pp. **ELM**.

1946. "Severe drought due in area in 1946-'47. Heavy rainfall predicted for next year." *Advertiser-Tribune*, Tiffin. 10 July, p. _. (Based on News Release, B.G.S.U., July 1946. Typewritten, 2 pp.). Ken H. McFall. [Not located in the newspaper].

1946. "Diet, droughts keep retired Bee Gee scientist happy as long-range predictions materialize. Dr. Moseley at 81 continues study of tree rings." *Toledo Sunday Times*, 20 October, p. 23; (Based on News Release, B.G.S.U., 19 October 1946. Typewritten, 3 pp.). Paul W. Jones. [Not located in the newspaper].

1946. "Tree rings reveal this section [central Ohio] is in for drought." *Columbus Citizen*, 20 October, p. 38. Don Strouse.

1946. "Drouths, proper diet keep B.G.S.U. educator healthy." *Columbus Dispatch*, 27 October, p. 2A.

1947. "What will the weather be? Here's a limited forecast for 1947 based on the records made in a few states 90.4 years ago." *Cappers Farmer* 58(February):16. **ELM**.

1947. "Long-time weather forecast. The 90.4-year cycle applied to old records form the basis for long-range predictions." *Cappers Farmer* 58(March):36. **ELM**.

1947. "Heavy spring rains reverse Dr. Moseley. Local scientist states meager records of 1857 weather are responsible." *Daily Sentinel-Tribune*, Bowling Green, 22 May, p. 1. (Based in part on News Release, B.G.S.U., 19 October 1946. Typewritten, 3 pp.). Paul W. Jones.

1948. "Ohio's tree-ring authority predicts record 1950 drought." *Cleveland Plain Dealer*, 4 January, p. 15-A. (Written by **ELM** especially for International News Special Service: His last known article on the subject).

1948. "Neither drought nor flood to seriously affect corn belt. Dr. Moseley claims." *Sandusky Register Star-News*, 10 April, p. 1. (Based on News Release, B.G.S.U., 10 April 1948. Typewritten, 2 pp.) Paul W. Jones.

1948. "Tree rings indicate sky's short of sap, biologist predicts drought for midwest." *Detroit News*, 20 May, p. _. [Page number not verified].

1948. "Weather repeats every 90 years, lifetime of research showed. Tree rings studied in theory that weather moves in cycles." *Columbus Citizen*, 28 November, p. 8B. Mervin Roland.

1948. "[Long range weather forecasts, predicts drought in 2037]." In "Dr. E. L. Moseley's life one of great achievements. . ." *Daily Sentinel-Tribune*, Bowling Green, 7 June, p. 2. [Ivan E. Lake].

1948. "Dr. Moseley's scientific findings had wide range. BGSU educator best known for extended weather forecasts based on tree growth." *Toledo Blade*, 7 June, p. 24.

1948. "Dr. Edwin Moseley, BGU scientist, dies. Acclaim won for system of predicting periods of floods, drought." *Toledo Times*, 7 June, pp. 1, 2.

1952. "[If living today, Dr. Edwin Lincoln Moseley would predict Lake Erie beach erosion in 1966]." News Release, B.G.S.U., 28 June 1952. Typewritten. 2 pp. Paul W. Jones.

1973. "Geologist [Moseley] predicted Erie flooding in 1904. Port Clinton under water by 2050?" *Sandusky Register*, 16 February, pp.15-16. Abner John Katzman.

1973. "Lake levels didn't stump him [Moseley], trees clue to heavy rains." [Name of newspaper not known]. Rochester, New York, 20 May, p. 4.

1973. Predicting Lake levels. *Inland Seas* 29(3): 182-185. Charles E. Frohman.

1973. Scientist foresaw shoreline erosion. *Echoes* 12(4): 7.

LISTS

OF THE

Birds, Mammals,

Birds' Eggs,

AND

Desiderata of Michigan Birds

IN THE

MUSEUM

OF THE

Kent Scientific Institute,

GRAND RAPIDS, MICH.

BY

E. L. MOSELEY, A. M.,
CURATOR OF THE MUSEUM.

Title page from Moseley's book, *Lists of the Birds, Mammals, Birds' Eggs, ... of the Kent Scientific Institute, Grand Rapids, Mich.* (1887).

VII. Contributions to Ornithology   Archive No. 1066
(Population Variations, Bob-White, and Blue Herons)

1887. *Lists of the birds, mammals, birds' eggs, and desiderata of Michigan birds in the Museum of the Kent Scientific Institute, Grand Rapids, Mich[igan]*. Grand Rapids, Michigan. 32 pp., 1 plate. **ELM**.

1891. Descriptions of two new species of flycatchers from the Island of Negros, Philippines. *The Ibis*. Sixth Series 3(9): 46-47, plate II. **ELM**. [Plate II reprinted as frontispiece to Niederhofer and Stuckey (1998); also p. 29, this book].

1893. "[Note on seeing no less than 50 kinds of birds in or near Sandusky on Saturday, 6 May 1893]." *Sandusky Register*, 8 May, p. 4.

1894. "A rare treasure added to Professor Moseley's collection at the high school." *Sandusky Sunday Register*, 18 February, p. 1.

1895. "Eagles in northern Ohio. They live on fish almost exclusively and are protected by law." *Sandusky Weekly Journal*, 19 January, p. 8; *Erie County Reporter*, 24 January, p. 5.

1895. The white headed eagle in northern Ohio. *American Naturalist* 29: 168-170. (Also, *Sandusky Weekly Journal,* 6 April, p. 8). **ELM**.

1896. "Protect the birds. A letter sent out to superintendents of schools." *Sandusky Register*, 16 April, p. 5. **ELM**.

1896. "One more Moseley kingfisher." *Sandusky Register*, 15 December, p. 9.

1897. A bird [brünnich's murre, *Uria lomvia*] new to Ohio. *Fifth Annual Report Ohio State Academy Science* 1896: 50. **ELM**.

1898. The white headed eagle in northern Ohio. *The Lakeside Magazine* 4(2): 36. (Reprinted by Eleanor Durr. 1984. Heritage Notes. Eagles—as observed by Professor Moseley, *Peninsular News*, 26 April). **ELM**.

1900. Occasional abundance of certain birds on or near Lake Erie. *The Lakeside Magazine* 6(4): 29-30. **ELM**.

1900. Occasional abundance of certain birds on or near Lake Erie. *Eighth Annual Report Ohio State Academy of Science* 1899: 12-15; also *Proceedings*. **ELM**.

1901. Old squaw ducks (not "pintails") caught in deep water fish nets. *Ninth Annual Report Ohio State Academy of Science* 1900: 19-20; also *Proceedings*. **ELM**.

1904. "Our birds. Prof. Moseley's splendid museum in the high school—affords students rare opportunities to study them." *Sandusky Register*, 4 March, p. 3.

1907. "Ornithological treasures. Mr. Moseley receives [an albatross] from New York the most important to his bird collection that has been made for years." *Sandusky Register*, 4 March, p. 3.

1907. "Many birds of many kinds in the high school museum . . . nearly seven hundred exhibits, . . ." *Sandusky Register*, 12 May, p. 12. **ELM**.

1907. "Birds are here in big numbers. Sixty-one varieties seen by Prof. Moseley and high [school] pupils on stroll Monday." *Sandusky Register*, 14 May, p. 5.

1912. Gull pensioners. *Bird Lore* 14(6): 338-341. **ELM**.

1912. "Many birds of many kinds in the high school museum. Inspection of collection shows nearly seven hundred exhibits, which public may view for last time this season, . . ." *Sandusky Register*, 12 March, p. 12. **ELM**.

1914. Wild fowl at Sandusky Bay in 1756 [Commentary on Moseley's paper, Gull pensioners]. *Bird Lore* 16(2): 114-115. Milo H. Miller. (Also, *Sandusky Register*, 11 April, p. 7).

1917. "Many birds on Catawba Island." *Sandusky Register*, 27 May, p. 12. **ELM**.

1920. "The return of the birds." *Sandusky Register*, 1 May, p. 3. **ELM**.

1924. "Says Vermilion eagle of 'bald' species, quite common near Sandusky." *Sandusky Register*, 7 December, p. 9. **[ELM]**.

1926. "Moseley will exhibit rare Hawaiian birds at museum . . ." *Sandusky Register*, 4 December, p. 3.

1927. "High [school] museum has relic passenger pigeon days." *Sandusky Register*, 30 April, p. 3. **ELM**.

1927. "Moseley says quail do good turn for farmers. Gives bob white credit for big decrease in number of potato bugs." *Sandusky Register*, 15 September, p. 5. **[ELM]**.

1927. Bob whites eliminate potato bugs. *School Science and Mathematics* 27. 813. **[ELM]**. (An item which quotes portions of Moseley's article in the *Toledo Blade*).

1928. "Local museum to exhibit specimen of crocodile bird." *Sandusky Register*, 22 March, p. 5. **ELM**.

1928. "Hummingbird collection is High [school] museum feature. Public invited to view 50 varieties . . ." *Sandusky Register*, 24 March, p. 3.

1928. "Identify [Cedar] Point bird visitors. E. L. Moseley describes kinglet's peculiarities." *Sandusky Register*, 26 October, p. 10.

1928. The abundance of woodpeckers and other birds in northeastern Louisiana. *Wilson Bulletin* 40(2): 115-116. New Series 35(143). **ELM**.

1928. Bob-white and the scarcity of potato beetles. *Wilson Bulletin* 40(3): 149-151. New Series 35(144). **ELM**.

*1928. Bob-white useful to the potato grower. *Potato Association of America Proceedings Fifteenth Annual Meeting*, Dec. 1928. pp. 259-262. **ELM**.

1929. Bob-white and scarcity of potato beetles. *School Science and Mathematics* 29: 196-198. **ELM**.

1929. "Rare specimens of birds are on display at museum . . ." *Sandusky Register*, 9 March, p. 3.

1930. Fluctuation of bird life with change in water level. *Wilson Bulletin* 42(3): 191-193. *New Series* 37(152). **ELM**.

1930. Abundance of the Golden Plover in Ohio in 1930. *Wilson Bulletin* 42(3): 292-293. *New Series* 37(152). **ELM**.

1930. "E. L. Moseley finds quail useful in work of potato beetle control." *Sandusky Register*, 23 December, p. 9. S. F. Hinkle, farm editor.

1930. "High water in Sandusky marshes results in big increase in wild fowl." *Sandusky Star-Journal*, 22 November, p. 3. **ELM**.

1931. The heronries of northern Ohio. (Abstract). *Ohio Journal of Science* 31(4): 270. **ELM**.

1932. "B[owling] G[reen] members [including E. L. Moseley] attend Ornithological meet." *Bee Gee News* 17(3): 1-6. 6 December.

1936. Blue Heron colonies in northern Ohio. *Wilson Bulletin* 48(1): 3-11. New Series 43(174). **ELM**.

1936. Starlings bathing in ice water. *Wilson Bulletin* 48(1): 310. New Series 43(178). **ELM**.

1936. Pugnacious cardinals. *Wilson Bulletin* 48(4): 312. New Series 43(178). **ELM**.

1938. Shore birds attracted to streams polluted by sewage. *Wilson Bulletin* 50(3): 204-205. New Series 45(185). **ELM**.

1943. Gyrfalcon in Ohio. *The Auk* 60(4): 598 + plate 14. **ELM**.

*1946. Variations in the bird population of Ohio and nearby states. *Ohio Journal of Science* 46: 308-322. **ELM**.

1946. "Barn owl is useful says Dr. E. L. Moseley." *Daily Sentinel-Tribune*, Bowling Green, 15 June, p. 1; "Farmer, spare that barn owl, it's a friend, Professor [Moseley] pleads." *Cleveland Plain Dealer*, 16 June, p. _. [Not located in the newspaper].

1946. "Noted B. G. scientist pleads for barn owl. Bird helps conserve food by eating mice, sparrows." [Newspaper not identified].

1946. Useful farm bird the barn owl. *Ohio Conservation Bulletin* 10(7): 30. **ELM**.

1947. Variations in the bird population of the north-central states due to climatic and other changes. *The Auk* 64(1): 15-35 + plate 4. **ELM**.

Upper: *Cryptolopha nigrorum*; **Lower:** *Abrornis olivacea*, **the two species of flycatchers from the Island of Negros, Philippines, named by Moseley.**

(*The Ibis*, Sixth Series 3: 46, 47, pl. II. 1891; Stuckey Collection)

NEW-WORLD SCIENCE SERIES
Edited by John W. Ritchie

TREES, STARS AND BIRDS

A Book of Outdoor Science

by

EDWIN LINCOLN MOSELEY, A.M.

*Head of the Science Department
State Normal College of
Northwestern Ohio*

ILLUSTRATED IN COLORS
*from paintings by Louis Agassiz Fuertes
and with photographs and drawings*

Yonkers-on-Hudson, New York
WORLD BOOK COMPANY
1919

Title page from Moseley's book, *Trees, Stars and Birds* (1919).

VIII. Contributions to Science Education & General Science
(Outdoor Science Teaching)

Archive No. 1067

1896. Science. pp. 416-418. *In* Do the public schools give a reasonable mastery of the subjects studied? *Ohio Educational Monthly* 45: 410-420. **ELM**.

1902. Original work for the high-school teacher. *School Science* 2: 188. Reported by L. Murbach. (Also, *Sandusky Daily Star*, 4 June, p. 3. Abstract of paper read at meeting of the Michigan School Masters' Club, Ann Arbor).

1902. "Original work for the high school teacher. A paper by Prof. E. L. Moseley, read at an Ann Arbor (Mich.) Teacher's Meeting, last spring." *Sandusky Daily Star*, 20 December, p. 5. **ELM**.

1903. Original work in high schools. *Ohio Educational Monthly* 52: 367-374. **ELM**.

1912. Some ways of teaching pupils practical hygiene. *School Science and Mathematics* 12: 1-5. **ELM**.

1917. Fifty-three years a teacher [Job Fish]. *Ohio Education Monthly* 66: 255-256. (Also, *Sandusky Daily Register*, 22 July, p. 7). **ELM**.

*1919. *Trees, Stars, and Birds: A Book of Outdoor Science*. World Book Co., Yonkers-on-Hudson, New York. 404 pp. Reprinted, 1921, 1922, 1924, 1925, 1927; Revised Edition, 1935. 418 pp.) **ELM**. (Reviews, *Sandusky Star-Journal*, 24 January, p. 11; J. T. Nichols. *Bird Lore* 21(2): 117. 1919; Carroll L. Fenton. *American Midland Naturalist* 7: 159-160, 1921).

1921. Seeing and understanding. *Ohio Educational Monthly* 70: 46-48. (Also, *Bee Gee News* 2(1): 1,3,20 January; *Sandusky Register*, 6 February, p. 5; *Toledo Naturalists Association Bulletin* 1(10): 1,4. 1947). **ELM**.

1924. A plea for more outdoor science teaching. *School Science and Mathematics* 24: 151-155. (Also, *Toledo Naturalists Association Bulletin* 1(2): [1, 4.] 1946). **ELM**.

1924. "Echoes from the science excursions." *Bee Gee News* 5(10): 6. 23 July.

1925. *Supplement to Trees, Stars, and Birds: With Key to Trees*. World Book Co., Yonkers-on-Hudson, New York. 29 pp. **ELM**. [Not available in the Library of the Hayes Presidential Center].

1925. Some suggestions for outdoor science teaching. *Elementary School Journal* 26: 58-66. (Notice of article published in *Sandusky Register*, 30 May, p. 10; excerpt published in *The American Schoolmaster* 2: 225-226; excerpt published under title "Moseley finds many children do not know from where milk comes, also lumber; urges nature study," in *Sandusky Star-Journal*, 13 October p. 2). **ELM**.

1927. *Our Wild Animals*. D. Appleton and Co., New York. 310 pp. **ELM**. (Reviews, *Sandusky Register*, 4 September, p. 7; Charles M. Turton. *School Science and Mathematics* 7: 159-160, 1927).

1937. Anecdotes from Moseley classes. *Daily Sentinel-Tribune*, Bowling Green. [on poison ivy], 1 April, p. 5; [on falling asleep in the classroom], 3 April, p. 5; [on proper identification of two mint plants], 5 April, **p. 5**; [on giving final exams to absentee athletes], 6 April, p. 8. Ivan E. Lake.

1938. *Biology for Life: A Workbook and Laboratory Manual for Use with any Biology Textbook*. College Entrance Book Co., Inc., New York. 312 pp. (Revised Edition, 1941. 316 pp.). **ELM**. [Not available in the Library of the Hayes Presidential Center].

1959. The physical sciences: Chemistry, Geology, Physics. Fifty years has wrought great changes... *Bowling Green State University Magazine* 4(2): 11-12. May. Clare S. Martin.

1974. "Moseley experiment in gravity." *In* Charles E. Frohman, *Sandusky Potpourri*, Item 37. The Ohio Historical Society, [Columbus]. 1974.

1985. "Remembering Mr. Bones. He used to be a key connection in learning about the body." *Sandusky Register*, 8 December, p. A-4.

NEW-WORLD SCIENCE SERIES
Edited by John W. Ritchie

TREES, STARS *and* BIRDS
A BOOK OF OUTDOOR SCIENCE

By Edwin Lincoln Moseley
Head of the Science Department, State Normal College of Northwestern Ohio

THE usefulness of nature study in the schools has been seriously limited by the lack of a suitable textbook. It is to meet this need that *Trees, Stars, and Birds* is issued. The author is one of the most successful teachers of outdoor science in this country. He believes in field excursions, and his text is designed to help teachers and pupils in the inquiries that they will make for themselves.

The text deals with three phases of outdoor science that have a perennial interest, and it will make the benefit of the author's long and successful experience available to younger teachers.

The first section deals with trees, and the discussion of maples is typical: the student is reminded that he has eaten maple sugar; there is an interesting account of its production; the fact is brought out that the sugar is really made in the leaves. The stars and planets that all should know are told about simply and clearly. The birds commonly met with are considered, and their habits of feeding and nesting are described. Pertinent questions are scattered throughout each section.

The book is illustrated with 167 photographs, 69 drawings, 9 star maps, and with 16 color plates of 58 birds, from paintings by Louis Agassiz Fuertes.

It is well adapted for use in junior high schools, yet the presentation is simple enough for pupils in the sixth grade.

Cloth. viii + 404 + xvi pages. Price $1.80.

WORLD BOOK COMPANY
Yonkers-on-Hudson, New York
2126 Prairie Avenue, Chicago

Advertisement for Moseley's book, *Trees, Stars and Birds* (1919).

(Gift of William R. Burk; Stuckey Collection)

OUR WILD ANIMALS

BY

EDWIN LINCOLN MOSELEY

HEAD OF THE SCIENCE DEPARTMENT
IN THE STATE NORMAL COLLEGE
OF NORTHWESTERN OHIO; AUTHOR
OF "TREES, STARS AND BIRDS"

ILLUSTRATED

NEW YORK
D. APPLETON AND COMPANY

Title page from Moseley's book, *Our Wild Animals* (1927).

IX. Contributions to Zoology [other than Ornithology]
(Mammals, Snakes, and other Animals)

Archive No. 1068

Mammals

1906. Notes on the former occurrence of certain mammals in northern Ohio. *Ohio Naturalist* 6: 504-505. **ELM**.

1915. "Prof. Moseley comments on bats' devotion to their young." *Sandusky Register*, 25 September, p. 5. [**ELM**].

1917. "Prof. Moseley writes of deer in Ohio." *Sandusky Star-Journal*, 24 May, p. 4. **ELM.**

1919. "Moseley writes about wild deer; also relates incidents regarding them while pets in Ohio . . ." *Sandusky Star-Journal*, 17 March, p. 9. [**ELM**].

1919. "Rare specimen of weasel here. Prof. Moseley writes interestingly of little, bloodthirsty animals." *Sandusky Star-Journal*, 22 March, p. 9. [**ELM**].

1921. "Traits of black bear told by Prof. Moseley; one hunter killed 100." *Sandusky Star-Journal*, 2 April, p. 6. **ELM**.

1924. "Margaretta wolf is coyote, declares Prof. E. L. Moseley who tells of habits of animals." *Sandusky Star-Journal*, 29 March, pp. 1,11.

1925. "Prof. Moseley, here for opening of high [school] museum; . . . tells about appetite of his opossum." *Sandusky Star-Journal*, 21 November, p.10.

*1927. *Our Wild Animals*. D. Appleton and Co., New York. 310 pp. **ELM**. (Reviews, *Sandusky Register*, 4 September, 1927, p. 7; Charles M. Turton. *School Science and Mathematics* 7: 159-160. 1927).

1928. Red bat as a mother. *Journal of Mammalogy* 9(3): 248-249. **ELM**.

1928. The number of young red bats in one litter. *Journal of Mammalogy* 9(3): 249. **ELM**.

1929. "Huge beast once roamed over this part of state. High [School] Museum . . . will exhibit interesting mammal specimens." *Sandusky Register*, 13 April, p. 5.

1929. "Bison bones found in this section remind that buffalo once roamed northern Ohio." *Sandusky Sunday Register*, 5 May, p. 7.

1930. Feeding a short-tailed shrew. *Journal of Mammalogy* 11(2): 224-225. **ELM**.

1930. "Woodchuck is one of specimens to be seen at museum Sunday." *Sandusky Register*, 6 December, p. 7.

1931. "Prof. Moseley tells about opossums and exhibits live one at museum." *Sandusky Star-Journal*, 5 December, p. 2. **ELM**.

1932. "Moselians travel to see elephants [guided by Roger Conant]." *Bee Gee News* 17(8): 1,4.

1934. Increase of badgers in northwestern Ohio. *Journal of Mammalogy* 15(2):156-158. **ELM**.

Snakes

1901. The python [*Python natalensis*] in Pennsylvania. *Science*. New Series 14: 852-853. **ELM**.

1909. "Prof. Moseley says venomous snakes are almost extinct in Erie County." *Sandusky Star-Journal*, 4 September, p. 6. **[ELM]**.

1911. "Don't kill the fox snake: Head of High School Department makes plea for useful reptile." *Sandusky Weekly Register*, 17 May, p. 10. **ELM**.

1914. "Few poisonous snakes found in this section; some specimens, like ribbon snake, are oddities." *Sandusky Star-Journal*, 10 June, p. 6. **ELM**.

1919. "Snakes? There aren't many of the venomous kind now, says Moseley." [Also, commentary on trembles and milk sickness]. *Sandusky Register,* 26 April, p. 12. **[ELM]**.

1931. "Prof. Moseley tells of another snake of python family found close to Lake [Erie]." *Sandusky Star-Journal*, 25 July, p. 5. **[ELM]**.

Other Animals

1905. "Our Museum. [Some animals]," p. 10 *In. Sandusky Register,* 16 June, pp. 9-10. Carroll C. Page.

1906. "A nice fat boa con[strictor]. A shark's man-eating jaw, the sword from a sword fish and some small katzenjammer cockroaches are among the interesting things to be seen at the high school museum." *Sandusky Star-Journal*, 30 January, p. 2.

1911. Housekeepers' interest in gill-netted fish. *The Ohio Farmer* 127: 630-631. 20 May. (Also, *Sandusky Register*, 20 May, p. 4, 1911.) **ELM**.

1921. "Eels placed in Lake Erie 40 years ago are caught. Thrive, but do not breed in fresh water—Ohio scientist traces their origin back to transparent ribbon of the sea." *Toledo Blade*, 22 April, p. 6. **ELM**.

1921. "Eels placed in Lake Erie 40 years ago are caught." *Sandusky Star-Journal*, 23 April, p. 2. **ELM**.

1923. *Gonorhynchus moseleyi*, a new species of herring-like fish from Honolulu. *Journal of the Washington Academy of Sciences* 13(15): 347-350. David Starr Jordan and John Otterbein Snyder.

1923. "New fish named in Moseley's honor." *Bee Gee News* 5(3): 7, (reprinted in *School Science and Mathematics* 24: 523. 1924).

1928. "Lamprey [*Petromyzon marinus*] brought to fishery here is placed in Moseley collection." *Sandusky Star-Journal*, 5 December, p. 13.

1928. "Thousands of specimens at high [school] museum today; ... Prof. Moseley identifies strange lamper eel." *Sandusky Register,* 9 December, p. 10.

1929. "Prof. E. L. Moseley discusses kinds and peculiarities of sharks; specimens in Museum." *Sandusky Star-Journal*, 5 March, p. 5. **ELM**.

1932. "Prof. Moseley to have [on] exhibit live termites at school museum Sunday." *Sandusky Star-Journal*, 5 March, p. 3.

1932. "Local museum open today and many expected. Exhibits of fairy shrimps and live termites will be on display ... at the high school museum under the direction of Prof. E. L. Moseley of Bowling Green State College." *Sandusky Register*, 6 March, p. 12.

Numbers and Years of Publications for Each Discipline in Books and Archival Periodicals

Discipline	Publications Total	Major	General Years of Study	Concentrated Years of Study	Discussed in Chapter
Astronomy	8	1	1903-1933		11
Botany	18	2	1895-1938	1889-1899	9
Geology	16	2	1895-1905	1894-1905	9
Health and Hygiene	10	0	1910-1912		—
Medical Science	8	2	1906-1917, 1941	1904-1917	9
Climatology; Meteorology	22	4	1897-1947	1928-1948	10
Ornithology	34	2	1887-1947		9
Science Education and General Science	12	1	1896-1925, 1938		11
Zoology (other than Ornithology)	22	1	1906-1934		9
Totals	150	15			

Note: This table was originally published in the Moseley Book by Niederhofer and Stuckey (1998, p. 100; for full citation, see p. 67 of this book). The total number of publications by Moseley for each discipline has been revised in this table by totaling the number of citations identified as written by him, or those citations with **ELM** in bold type. The number of major publications for each discipline remains the same here as in the above-cited Moseley Book. Those publications chosen for this "major" status are identified in this book with an asterisk placed by the year of publication for each chosen citation. The right-most column of numbers refers to the respective chapters in the Niederhofer-Stuckey Moseley Book that discusses Moseley's publications for each discipline.

Membership in Professional Scientific Organizations and Summation of Publications in Periodicals

A. Activities in Organizations and Publication Summation

American Association for the Advancement of Science (New York City)
Member, 1885; Fellow, 1902; Papers Read at Meetings, one in 1896;
Fifty Year Member, 1937, one of 37 who was a member for 50 or more years.

	*Numbers of Publications
Published Papers:	
Science, 1896, 1901	2

American Society of Mammalogists (Baltimore)
Charter Member, 1919
Published Papers:

Journal of Mammalogy, 1928(2)**, 1930, 1934	4

Central Association of Science and Mathematics Teachers (Chicago)
Papers Read at Meetings, one in 1923
Published Papers:

School Science, 1902	1
School Science and Mathematics, 1912, 1924, 1929, 1938	4

Chicago Academy of Sciences (Chicago)
Elected Honorary Life Member, 1945

Field Naturalists Association (Toledo)
Charter Member, 1932; Honorary Member
Published Papers:

Toledo Naturalists Association, Annual Bulletin (Toledo, Ohio), 1939, 1947; 2 reprinted articles, 1946, 1947	2

Michigan Academy of Science (Lansing); name changed to Michigan Academy of Science, Arts, and Letters (Ann Arbor)
Member, 1905; Chairman for the Botanical Section, 1934-1935
Papers Read at Meetings, five during the years 1905, 1930, 1935 (Chairman), 1939, 1943
Published Papers:

39

        Annual Reports, 1905   1
        Papers of the Michigan Academy of Science, Arts,
            and Letters 1931, 1940, 1941   3

The Ohio State Academy of Science (Columbus); 1913 name changed to The Ohio Academy of Science

Charter Member, 1891, Secretary, 1895-1903; President, 1904; Elected Honorary Life Member, 1943

Papers Read at Meetings, 33 papers read during the years from 1894 through 1939

    Published Papers:
        Annual Report, 1895-1905   10
        Ohio Journal of Science, 1931, 1939, 1946   3
        Ohio Naturalist, 1906   2
        Special Papers, 1899, 1928, 1941   3
        Annual Report, Reports of Meetings by
            the Secretary, 1896-1904   16

Wilson Ornithological Club (Sioux City)

Member, 1925; Vice-President, 1932-1933
    Published Papers:
        Wilson Bulletin 1928(2), 1930(2), 1936(3), 1938   8

B. Publication Summation by Topics in Periodicals not Affiliated with Professional Organizations; or if affiliated, then Moseley not known to be a member

Astronomy; Meteorology
    Popular Astronomy (Northfield, Minnesota), 1904, 1944   2
    Journal of the Royal Astronomical Society of Canada (Toronto), 1941   1
    Monthly Weather Review (Washington, D.C.), 1903   1
    American Fruit Grower (Cleveland), 1945   1
    Scientific American (New York City), 1931   1

Botany
    Botanical Gazette (Crawfordsville, Indiana), 1896   1
    American Naturalist (Philadelphia), 1897   1

Geology
    National Geographic Magazine (Washington, D.C.), 1902, 1903 (2)   3

Medical Science
Medical Record (New York), 1909, 1910, 1917	3
Mulford's Veterinary Bulletin (Philadelphia), [not located], 1909	1

Ornithology
The Ibis (London), 1891	1
Bird Lore (New York), 1912, 1914	2
The Auk (Lancaster, PA), 1943, 1947	2
American Naturalist (Philadelphia) 1897	1

Science Education
Elementary School Journal (Chicago), 1925	1
American Schoolmaster (Ypsilanti, Michigan), 1925	1
Ohio Educational Monthly (Columbus), 1896, 1903 (2), 1917, 1921	5
Bee Gee News (Bowling Green, Ohio), 1921, 1925	2

C. Publication Summation in Popular and Literary Periodicals
Cappers Farmer (Topeka, Kansas), 1947 (2)	2
Ohio Conservation Bulletin (Columbus), 1946	1
Country Gentleman (Philadelphia), 1943	1
Lakeside Magazine (Lakeside, Ohio), 1898 (2), 1899, 1900	4
Ohio Farmer (Cleveland), 1910 (3), 1911 (4), 1912	8

D. Newspapers (cited most frequently)
Cleveland Plain Dealer
Daily Sentinel-Tribune (Bowling Green, Ohio)
Erie County Reporter
Sandusky Daily-Star
Sandusky Register
Sandusky Star-Journal
Toledo Blade

Footnotes:

*   The numbers in this column refer to the number of papers published in the corresponding periodical.

**   The number in parenthesis refers to the number of times that particular year Moseley published a paper in that particular periodical.

Niederhofer and Stuckey Honored with Moseley Book Award

Paul Yon, Relda E. Niederhofer, Ronald L. Stuckey.

(Taken 6 April 2000 by Ann Bowers for RLS)

Relda E. Niederhofer of Sandusky, Ohio, and Ronald L. Stuckey of Columbus, Ohio, received the Local History Publication Award for their book, *Edwin Lincoln Moseley (1865-1948) Naturalist, Scientist, Educator* published in 1998 by RLS Creations, Columbus, Ohio. The award, given by the Center for Archival Collections of Bowling Green State University, Bowling Green, Ohio, recognizes authors for outstanding writing and publication in the subject of local history for northwestern Ohio. The judges described the Moseley book as "well researched and a well-written history of Ohio's greatest naturalist and educator."

Archives Director Paul Yon made the presentation to the authors at the Conference on Local History sponsored by the BGSU Archival Collections Center, held 6 April 2000 at the Holiday Inn, Perrysburg, Ohio. The authors were each presented a beautiful plaque and a modest monetary contribution. They each responded with a short commentary about how the project of Moseley's life and scientific work came to be a book.

OTHER CONTRIBUTIONS

I. Essays on Various Topics

A. Travels   Archive No. 1037

1892.   "Long's Peak at sunset and a night on the mountain." *Sandusky Register*, 25 November, [p. 2]; 26 November, [p. 2]; 28 November, [p. 3]; 29 November, [p. 2]. **ELM**.

1898.   "In Hong Kong. Scenes and conditions in the old Chinese City. Prof. Moseley's description." *Sandusky Star*, 2 August, p. 1. **ELM**.

1904.   "Stuart Hamilton. Prof. Moseley writes of his condition [of appendicitis] and rough experience on freight trains with tramps." *Sandusky Register*, 11 July, p. 5. In letter of 3 July 1904 to Carl Giebel, Sandusky, from Bloomington, Illinois. **ELM**.

1913.   "Lost" "[near Pioneer, Louisiana, 27 December 1912]." *The Fram*, [Sandusky High School] 12(3):6-8. 1913. January. **ELM**.

1922.   "Prof. Moseley tells of trip in far West." *Sandusky Register*, 25 June, p. 7. **ELM**.

1922.   "Prof. Moseley writes of beauty of Honolulu's parks, gardens; suggests plan for Sandusky." *Sandusky Star-Journal*, 19 August, p. 7. **ELM**.

1924.   The Hawaiian Islands as a summer resort. *School Science and Mathematics* 24:513-516. **ELM**.

1928.   The abundance of woodpeckers and other birds in northeastern Louisiana. *Wilson Bulletin* 40(2): 115-116. **ELM**.

B. Other Topics   Archive No. 1037

1894. "Slate writing. The mysterious trick of so-called spirit mediums." *Sandusky Register*, 11 December, p. 7. **ELM**.

1900. "[Prof. Moseley hosts merry party for Sandusky High School graduates attending or about to attend college]." *Sandusky Register*, 13 August, p. 2.

1901. Heights and distances in Sandusky. *Sandusky Star-Journal*, 14 December, p. 20. **ELM**.

1903. "The resources of Sandusky." *Sandusky Evening Star*, 19 November, p. 4. **ELM**.

1906. "New theory is advanced. Prof. Moseley discusses recent earthquake in golden state [California]. *Sandusky Register*, 29 April, p. 3. **ELM**.

C. Opinions and Editorials   Archive No. 1038

1911. "[The changing population of Sandusky]." *The Fram*, [Sandusky High School]. 11(2):3-4. December. **ELM**.

1912. "[Sandusky High School graduates willing to work]." *The Fram*, [Sandusky High School]. 11(3):6-7. January. **ELM**.

1912. "[Having definite pursuits in life]." *The Fram*, [Sandusky High School], 11(8):19-20. June. **ELM**.

1915. "Sandusky voters' great opportunity." *Sandusky Star-Journal*, 8 October, p. 4. **ELM**.

1918. "The value of a natural history museum." *Sandusky Register*, 1 June, p. 2. **ELM**.

1925. "Moseley finds many children do not know from whence milk comes, also lumber; urges nature study. *Sandusky Star-Journal*, 13 October, p. 2. **[ELM]**.

1942. How a good library may be useful in scientific research. Manuscript, Typewritten. 16 December. 2 pp. **ELM**.

II. Lists of Special Lectures

A. Delivered at the Sandusky High School   Archive No. 1039

15 February 1890 "On the Philippine Islands." *Sandusky Register*, 13 February 1890, p. 4. [Notice only].

22 November 1890. "What people eat and how they eat." *Sandusky Register*, 27 November 1890, p. 4. [Notice only].

5 December 1890. "Some popular delusions." *Sandusky Register*, 5 December, p. 4. [Notice only]. *Sandusky Register*, 6 December, p. 1. [Summary]. "More about Delusions: [Clean Air and Respiratory Diseases]." *Sandusky Weekly Register*, 16 December 1891, suppl., p. 6. [Summary].

30 January 1892. "Peculiar customs of the Malays, Mongolians and Americans." *Sandusky Register*, 1 February 1892, p. 4. [Notice only].

13 February 1892. "What we eat." *Sandusky Register*, 15 February 1892, p. 4; *Sandusky Weekly Register*, 17 February 1892, p. 5. [Summary].

18 December 1893. "Sanitary science." *Sandusky Register*, 15 December 1893, p. 2. [Notice only].

19 May 1899. "The Flora of the Islands and Sandusky's adjacent country." *Sandusky Register*, 21 May 1899, p. 5. [Notice only].

28 November 1900. "Sanitary science: Typhoid Fevers." *Sandusky Register*, 1 December 1900, p. 2. [Notice only].

5 December 1900. "Sanitary science: Consumption." *Sandusky Register*, 1 December 1900, p. 2. [Notice only].

— November 1903. "The resources of Sandusky." *Sandusky Evening Star*, 19 November 1903, p. 4. [Summary].

10 June 1903. "How to exterminate the mosquito." *Sandusky Star-Journal*, 10 June 1903, p. 6; *Sandusky Weekly Star*, 11 June 1903, p. 5; *Sandusky Register*, 11 June 1903, p. 2; *Sandusky Register*, 19 June 1903, p. 2. [Summaries].

29 October 1910. "The Philippines." *Sandusky Register*, 29 October 1910, p. 2. [Notice only].

21 April 1912. "Moseley discusses wonders of deep. Tells of animal and plant life to be found there. How icebergs are formed." *Sandusky Register*, 22 April 1912, p. 2. [Summary].

13 April 1930. "Hawaii lecture here on Sunday . . . in illustrated talk by Moseley." *Sandusky Star-Journal*, 12 April 1930, p. 12. [Notice only].

B. Delivered at Various Locations   Archive No. 1039

26 May 1898. "Philippine Islands." Young Men's Club, Grace Church Parish House, Sandusky, *Sandusky Register*, 27 May 1898, p. 5. Notice Only.

Summer 1903. "Physiographic features of the Sandusky region," Lake Laboratory on Cedar Point, Sandusky (*Lake Laboratory Announcement,* The Ohio State University, Columbus, 1903). Title only.

Summer 1903. "Collecting in the Philippine Islands," Lake Laboratory on Cedar Point, Sandusky (*Lake Laboratory Announcement*, The Ohio State University, Columbus, 1903). Title only.

7 May 1926. "The flora of Sandusky and vicinity and wild flower preservation." Carnegie Hall, Sandusky, *Sandusky Register*, 8 May 1926, p. 2. [Summary].

Sandusky High School, Sandusky, Ohio.

(Post Card No. 1187G. B. S. Stephens, Cleveland, Ohio; Stuckey Collection)

III. Titles of Papers Presented at Scientific Meetings
(citations provided for those papers published)*

A. Meetings of The Ohio Academy of Science   Archive No. 1070
1. Titles of Papers Presented and Published (1894-1939)

1891-1893.   No papers presented.

1894.   Title No. 6. "Notes on the bald eagle," (*Third Annual Report*, p. 46. 1895). [Title only].

1894.   The white headed eagle in northern *Ohio. American Naturalist* 29:168-170. 1895. (Also, *Sandusky Weekly Journal*, 6 April 1895, p. 8). **1066**.

1894.   The white headed eagle in northern Ohio. *The Lakeside Magazine* 4(2):36. 1898. (Reprinted by Eleanor Durr. 1984. Heritage Notes. Eagles—as observed by Professor Moseley, *Peninsular News*, 26 April). **1066**.

1894.   Title No. 22. "Attractions for a scientist in the vicinity of Sandusky," (*Third Annual Report*, p. 47. 1895). [Title only].

1894.   "Attractions for a scientist [in the vicinity of Sandusky]. Prof. Moseley's masterly paper before The [Ohio] Academy of Science." *Sandusky Register*, 30 December 1894, p. 5; *Sandusky Weekly Register*, 2 January 1895, p. 10. Attractions for a scientist in the vicinity of Sandusky. (Abstract). *Third Annual Report Ohio Academy of Science* 1895:5. 1895. **1061, 1062**.

1894.   Title No. 30. "Hygienic dangers of modern civilization," (*Third Annual Report*, p. 47. 1895). [Title only; paper not published].

1895.   Title No. 30. "Flora of Erie County and the islands," 20 min. (*Fifth Annual Report*, p. 9. 1897). [Title only].

1895.   "The plants and flowers of Erie County." *Sandusky Register*, 15 April 1896, p. 5; *Sandusky Weekly Register*, 22 April 1896, p. 5. **1061**.

1896.   Title No. 9. "A bird [Brünnich's murre, *Uria lomvia*] new to Ohio," (*Fifth Annual Report*, p. 12. 1897). [Title only].

Footnote:
* To locate a copy of a particular paper published by Moseley as cited for Archive Numbers 1070, 1072, and 1073, the user needs to consult the appropriate file of the Archive Number provided at the end of the published citation.

1896. A bird [Brünnich's Murre, *Uria lomvia*] new to Ohio. *Fifth Annual Report Ohio Academy Science* 1896:50. 1897. **1066**.

1897. Title No. 7. "Evidence as to the origin of the islands of Lake Erie." 20 min. (*Sixth Annual Report*, p. 9. 1898). [Title only].

1897. Lake Erie enlarging. The Islands separated from the mainland in recent times. *The Lakeside Magazine* 1(9):14-20. 1898. **1062**.

1897. Title No. 31. "Reversion of loments to leaves in the tick-trefoil," 2 min. *Sixth Annual Report*, p. 9. 1898). [Title only].

1897. Reversion of loments to leaves in ticktrefoil. *Sixth Annual Report Ohio Academy of Science* 1897:32 + discussion 32-34. 1898. **1061**.

1898. Title No. 33. "Some rare Ohio plants," 5 min. (*Seventh Annual Report*, p. 15. 1898). [Title only; paper not published].

1898. Title No. 47. "Climate of the Philippine Islands," 5 min.; Title No. 48. "Life in the Philippines," [time not given], (*Seventh Annual Report*, p. 16. 1899). [Titles only; papers not published].

1899. Title No. 19. "Occasional abundance of certain birds on or near Lake Erie." (*Eighth Annual Report*, p. 10. 1899). [Title only].

1899. Occasional abundance of certain birds on or near Lake Erie. *The Lakeside Magazine* 6(4):29-30. 1900. **1066**.

1899. Occasional abundance of certain birds on or near Lake Erie. *Eighth Annual Report Ohio Academy of Science* 1899:12-15; also *Proceedings* 7(4):12-15. 1900. **1066**.

1899. Title No. 43. "An extinct proboscidian engraved on stone by a contemporary artist. A unique specimen discovered in Sandusky County by H. A. Winters. To be exhibited at this meeting." 5 min. (*Eighth Annual Report*, p. 11. 1900). [Title only; paper not published].

1900. Title No. 18. "A rock valley crossing Huron and Erie counties." 15 min. (*Ninth Annual Report*, p. 14. 1901). [Title only].

1900. "Ancient rock valley [from Willard to east of Huron]." *Erie County Reporter*, 22 July 1909, p. 4. (Reprinted under the title "Moseley discovers ancient valley," *In* Charles E. Frohman. *Sandusky Area Miscellany*, Item 54. The Ohio Historical Society. [Columbus]. 1973). **1062**.

1900. Title No. 24. "Old-squaw-ducks (not "pintails") caught in deep water fish nets." 2 min. (*Ninth Annual Report*, p. 14. 1901). [Title only].

1900. Old squaw ducks (not "pintails") caught in deep water fish nets. *Ninth Annual Report Ohio Academy of Science* 1900:19-20; also *Proceedings* 3(1):19-20. 1901. **1066**.

1901. No paper presented.

1902. Title No. 18. "Additions and corrections to the Sandusky flora." 8 min. (*Eleventh Annual Report*, p. 14. 1902). [Title only].

1902. Additions and corrections to the Sandusky flora. (Abstract). *Eleventh Annual Report Ohio Academy of Science* 1902:27; also *Proceedings* 3(4):27. 1903. **1061**.

1902. Title No. 34. "Currents in Sandusky Bay," 8 min. (*Eleventh Annual Report*, p. 14. 1902). **1062**.

1902. "How the currents act in the Bay of Sandusky. Travelling bottles brought information to E. L. Moseley which he gave before the Ohio State Academy of Science." *Sandusky Register*, 1 December 1902, p. 5; *Sandusky Weekly Register*, 3 December 1902, p. 3. **1062**.

1902. The currents in Sandusky Bay. *Eleventh Annual Report Ohio Academy of Science* 1902:21-26. 1903. (Notice of this article printed in *Sandusky Register*, 29 November 1902, p. 3; *Sandusky Star-Journal*, 1 December 1902, p. 6). **1062**.

1902. Title No. 39. "The meteor of September 15th." 5 min. (*Eleventh Annual Report* p. 14. 1903). [Title only].

1902. The meteor of September 15, 1902. (Abstract). *Eleventh Annual Report Ohio Academy of Science* 1902:26. 1903; also *Proceedings* 3(4):26. 1903. **1060**.

1902. Meteor of September 15, 1902. *Popular Astronomy* 12:190-192. 1904. (Also, *Sandusky Register*, 19 March 1904, p. 9). **1060**.

1903. No paper presented.

1904. President's address. "The formation of Sandusky Bay and Cedar Point." (*Thirteenth Annual Report*, p. 177. 1905). [Title only]. **1062**.

1904. "President Moseley of Sandusky . . . told of the formation of Sandusky Bay and Cedar Point." *Sandusky Weekly Register*, 30 November, 1904, p. 4. **1062**.

1904. Formation of Sandusky Bay and Cedar Point. *Thirteenth Annual Report Ohio Academy of Science* 1904:179-238; also *Proceedings* 4:179-238. 1905. **1062**.

1904. "Sandusky Bay and Cedar Point: Their formation—the changes wrought by the hand of time. What the waters have covered in ages past—natures silent forces." *Sandusky Register*, 20 January 1906, pp. 9-12; *Sandusky Weekly Register*, 24 January 1906, pp. 13-16. (Reprinted under the title *Lake Erie: Floods, Lake Levels, Northeast Storms*. The Ohio Historical Society, Columbus. 64 pp. 1973). **1062**.

1905. Title No. 33. "The cause of trembles in cattle, sheep, and horses, and milk-sickness in man." 12 min. (*Fourteenth Annual Report*, p. 308. 1905). [Title only].

1905. "Says tremble-weed is cause of milk-sickness. Prof. Moseley is prepared to prove claim at anytime." *Sandusky Register*, 25 January 1906, p. 8. **1064**.

1905. The cause of trembles in cattle, sheep and horses and of milk-sickness in people. *Ohio Naturalist* 6:463-470, 477-483. 1906. (Also, *Sandusky Register*, 28 April 1906, pp. 9, 11; *Sandusky Weekly Register*, 9 May 1906, p. 10). **1064**.

1906-1908. No papers presented.

1909. Title No. 13. "Milk-sickness in Sandusky County during 1909." 10 min.; Title No. 27. "Buckeye poisoning," 8 min. (*Eighteenth Annual Report*, p. 325. 1910). [Titles only; papers not published].

1910-1913. No papers presented.

1914. Title No. 12. "The cause of milk sickness and trembles." 15 min. (*Proceedings Ohio Academy of Science* 6(4):172. 1920). [Title only].

1917. Milk sickness and trembles caused by resin of white snakeroot. *The Medical Record* 92:428. 1917. (Notice of this article published in *Sandusky Register*, 10 October 1917, p. 10). **1064**.

1915-1919. No papers presented.

OTHER CONTRIBUTIONS/TITLES OF PAPERS AT SCIENTIFIC MEETINGS

1920. Title No. 46. "Diastrophism still continuing in the Great Lakes region." 15 min. (*Proceedings Ohio Academy of Science* 7(5):148. 1920). [Title only].

1920. "Water deepening in lakes; Ohio scientist tells why." *Sandusky Star-Journal*, 17 July 1920, p. 8. **1062**.

1921. Title No. 23. "Diet of a captive mole." 5 min. (*Proceedings Ohio Academy of Science* 7(6):192. 1921.) [Title only; paper not published].

1922-1923. No papers presented.

1924. Title No. 14. "Pest hunts in Wood County." 10 min. (*Proceedings Ohio Academy of Science* 7(9):320. 1924). [Title only; paper not published].

1924. Title No. 89. "The peculiar flora of the sand region west of Toledo [Oak Openings]. 10 min. (*Proceedings Ohio Academy of Science* 7(9):323. 1924). [Title only].

1925-1926. No papers presented.

1927. Title No. 21. "The red bat as a mother." 6 min. (*Proceedings Ohio Academy of Science* 8(2):76. 1927). [Title only].

1927. Red bat as a mother. *Journal of Mammalogy* 9(3):248-249. 1928. **1068**.

1928. Flora of the Oak Openings west of Toledo. *Proceedings Ohio Academy of Science* 8:79-134. 1928. Special Paper No. 20. (Commentary by Jeanne Hawkins. Toledo Naturalist's Association Yearbook 24:45-48. 1968). **1061**.

1928-1929. No papers presented.

1930. Title No. 44. "Some plants in the flora of northern Ohio probably brought from the West by Indians. 12 min. (*Proceedings Ohio Academy of Science* 8)7):378. 1930). [Title only].

1930. Title No. 5. The heronries of northern Ohio. 12 min. (*Ohio Journal of Science* 31(4):270. 1931). [Abstract]. **1066**.

1930. Blue heron in northern Ohio. *Wilson Bulletin* 48(1):3-11. 1936. New Series 43(174). **1066**.

1931. Some plants that were probably brought to northern Ohio from the West by Indians. *Papers of the Michigan Academy of Science, Arts, and Letters* (1930) 13:169-172. 1931. (also, *Sandusky Register*, 15 March 1931, p. 10). **1061**.

1931-1937. No papers presented.

1938. Title No. 19. "The age factor in the diameter growth of rare white oaks." 15 min., charts. [Title only].

1939. Invitational presentation. "Prediction of floods on the Ohio River."

1939. Long time forecasts of Ohio River floods. *Ohio Journal of Science* 39(4):220-231. 1939. (*Biological Abstracts* 14:567. 1940). **1065**.

2. List of Moseley's Reports as Secretary   Archive No. 1071 of The Ohio Academy of Science (1895-1904)

1896. The Ohio Academy of Science. [Fourth Annual Summer Meeting, 2-3 July 1855]. *Fourth Annual Report Ohio State Academy of Science* 40-42; also *Ohio Educational Monthly* 44:408-409. 1898.

1897. Cincinnati Meeting [26-27 December 1895]. *Fifth Annual Report Ohio State Academy of Science* 7-9.

1897. Oxford Field Meeting [4-5 June 1896]. *Fifth Annual Report Ohio State Academy of Science* 10.

1897. Columbus Meeting [29-30 December 1896]. *Fifth Annual Report Ohio State Academy of Science* 10-13.

1898. Winter Meeting [28-29 December 1896]. *Sixth Annual Report Ohio State Academy of Science* 7-10.

1898. Field Meeting [28 May 1897]. *Sixth Annual Report Ohio State Academy of Science* 10-11.

1899. Winter Meeting [29-30 December 1898]. *Seventh Annual Report Ohio State Academy of Science* 9-16.

1899. Field Meeting [3-4 June 1898]. *Seventh Annual Report Ohio State Academy of Science* 16-17.

1900. Winter Meeting [22-23 December 1899]. *Eighth Annual Report Ohio State Academy of Science* 7-11.

1900. Summer Meeting [25 August 1899]. *Eighth Annual Report Ohio State Academy of Science* 12.

1901. Winter Meeting [26-27 December 1900]. *Ninth Annual Report Ohio State Academy of Science* 9-14.

1901. Summer Meeting [26-28 June 1900]. *Ninth Annual Report Ohio State Academy of Science* 15. (Also printed as a separate item. 3 pp.).

1902. Report of the Eleventh Annual Meeting of the Ohio State Academy of Science [29-30 November 1901]. *Tenth Annual Report Ohio State Academy of Science* 17-20.

1902. Field Meeting [31 May and 1 June 1901]. *Tenth Annual Report Ohio State Academy of Science* 21.

1903. Report of the Twelfth Annual Meeting of the Ohio State Academy of Science [28-29 November 1902]. *Eleventh Annual Report Ohio State Academy of Science* 11-14.

1904. Report of the Thirteenth Annual Meeting of the Ohio State Academy of Science [27 November 1903]. *Proceedings of the Ohio State Academy of Science* 4:9-11. [*Twelfth Annual Report Ohio State Academy of Science*].

B. Meetings of The Michigan Academy of Science, Arts, and Letters

Archive No. 1072

30, 31 March, 1 April 1905. "Changes of Level at the West End of Lake Erie." Eleventh Annual Meeting, Ann Arbor. (*Seventh Report of the Michigan Academy of Science*, pp. 38-39. 1905). Abstract. **1062**.

20-22 March 1930. "Some plants in the flora of northern Ohio which were probably brought from the West by Indians." Section Botany. Thirty-Fifth Annual Meeting, Ann Arbor. (*Papers of the Michigan Academy of Science, Arts, and Letters* (1930) 13:169-172. 1931; *Sandusky Register*, 15 March 1931, p. 10.) Complete Paper. **1061**.

7-9 March, 1 April 1935. "Prof. Moseley presides at Michigan Meeting." *Bee Gee News* 19(25): 1. 20 March. **1072**.

16-18 March 1939. "The ninety-year precipitation cycle." Section Geology and Mineralogy. Forty-First Annual Meeting, Ann Arbor. (*Papers of the Michigan Academy of Science, Arts, and Letters.* (1939) 25:491-496.1940). Complete Paper. **1065**.

26, 27 March 1943. "Prospects for insufficient rain 1943 to 1947." Section Botany. Forty-Eighth Annual Meeting, Ann Arbor. (*Papers of the Michigan Academy of Science, Arts, and Letters* (1943) 29:23-29. 1944). Complete Paper. **1065**.

C. Meetings of Other Organizations   Archive No. 1073

25 August 1896. "A comparison of the flora of Erie County, Ohio with that of Erie County, New York." The American Association for the Advancement of Science, Buffalo, New York. (*Proceedings of the American Association for the Advancement of Science* 45: 186. 1897. January). Frederic Ward Putnam. Title only; A comparison of the flora of Erie Co., Ohio, with that of Erie Co., N.Y. Abstract. (*Science*, new series 4: 434; *Botanical Gazette* 22: 224. 1896). **ELM**. Complete Paper. **1061**.

28 March 1902. "Original Work for the High School Teacher [Mapping the Channels of Sandusky Bay]." Michigan School Masters Club, Ann Arbor. (*School Science* 2:188. 1902.). Abstract. (*Sandusky Daily Star*, 20 December 1902, p. 5). Complete Paper. **1062**.

March 1909. "The Cause of Trembles and Milksickness." The Erie County (Ohio) Medical Society, Sandusky, Ohio. (*The Medical Record* 75:839-844). Complete Paper. **1064**.

1 December 1923. "A Plea for More Outdoor Science Teaching." Central Association of Science and Mathematics Teachers, Indianapolis, Indiana. (*School Science and Mathematics* 24:151-155. 1924). Complete Paper. **1067**.

IV. Local Field Excursions by Moseley's Classes from the Sandusky High School, 1891-1914, by Various Writers and Editors

Archive No. 1014

1891. "[Botany class takes trip to Johnson's Island]." *Sandusky Register*, 19 May, p. 4. Notice Only.

1893. "[Botany class takes trips to Cedar Point, Castalia Blue Hole, Magaretta Ridge, and woods in Sandusky County]." *Sandusky Register*, 25 May, p. 1. Grace Farwell, editor.

1893. "[Botany and zoology classes take trips to various places near Sandusky and to the Huron River about two and a half miles west of Milan]." *Sandusky Register*, 1 June, p. 4. Grace Farwell, editor.

1893. "[Botany class takes trip to Berlin Heights]." *Sandusky Register*, 5 October, p. 4. Jessie Hornig, editor. Notice Only.

1894. "[Botany class takes trip to Kelleys and Green Islands]." *Sandusky Register*, 17 May, p. 8. Notice Only.

1894. "[Botany class takes trip to Put-in-Bay Island]." *Sandusky Weekly Register*, 6 June, p. 7. Theresa Thorndale. Notice Only.

1894. "[Field excursion scheduled for Natural History students to the Erie Islands]." *Sandusky Sunday Register*, 1 July, p. 8. Notice Only.

1894. "[Moseley returns from 3-day botanical research trip on the Lake Erie Islands]." *Sandusky Register*, 4 August, p. 8. Notice Only.

1895. "[Moseley's classes in botany and geology go to Berlin community for day's outing]." *Erie County Reporter*, 25 April, p. 4.

1895. "One of our excursions [taken to Oberlin, Ohio]. Essay read before junior and senior class, Sandusky High School." *Sandusky Register*, 16 November, p. 6. Ralph H. McKelvey.

1896. "[Botany class takes trip to Milan]." *Sandusky Register*, 29 April, p. 3.

1896. "[Botany and zoology trip to Johnson's Island]." *Sandusky Sunday Register*, 3 May, p. 5. Notice Only.

1896.   "[Botany and natural history students take trip to Put-in-Bay Island]." *Sandusky Register*, 12 May, p. 6. Theresa Thorndale. Notice Only.

1897.   "Took wine with them to the High School botanical excursion in Margaretta. Disgraceful conduct on the part of several students who joined the excursion." *Sandusky Register*, 14 May, p. 8. (Also, the following items in the *Sandusky Register*, 20 May 1897, p. 5; 21 May 1897, p. 8; 22 May 1897, p. 5; 26 May 1897, p. 5; 27 May 1897, p. 4; 7 June 1897, p. 4). **ELM**.

1897.   "Day on the Huron's Banks. High School seniors took a trip that truly paid. Glowing account of an interesting expedition through miles of dust to a beautiful river." *Sandusky Register*, 27 September, p. 5.

1898.   "[Moseley and two students to explore caves at Put-in-Bay]." *Sandusky Weekly Register*, 16 March, p. 4. Theresa Thorndale.

1901.   "[Senior class goes on botanizing excursion to Berlin Heights]." *Sandusky Daily Star*, 18 May, p. 4. Notice Only.

1903.   "[Botany class takes trip to Berlin]." *Erie County Reporter*, 7 May, p. 4. Notice only.

1905.   "[Classes in physical geography enjoy delightful excursion to Berlin Heights under Mr. Moseley]." *The Fram*, [Sandusky High School]. 4(8): 28. June.

1914.   "[Biology class students, teachers, and other students explore Kelleys Island]." *The Fram*, [Sandusky High School]. 13(8): 30. June.

1914.   "[Students in Moseley's physical geography class, biology students, teachers, and guests take popular excursion to Put-in-Bay]." *The Fram*, [Sandusky High School]. 13(8): 30. June.

1924.   "Echoes from the science excursions." *Bee Gee News*, 5(10): 6. 23 July.

1930.   "Botany students enjoy trip to Catawba Island." *Bee Gee News*, 14(8): 3. 23 May.

V. The High School Museum at Sandusky, later moved to Bowling Green
Archive No. 1020
Contributed by Relda E. Niederhofer

1890. "[On forming a museum]." *Sandusky Register*, 29 September, p. 4; *Sandusky Register*, 18 October, p. 1; *Sandusky Register*, 6 December, p. 4.

1890. "Moseley to open museum at the high school." *Sandusky Weekly Register*, 31 December, p. 4.

1891. "An interesting exhibit. Prof. Moseley's collection of birds and shells at the high school building." *Sandusky Register*, 2 January, p. 4.

1891. "Moseley's museum open to public this afternoon." *Sandusky Register*, 31 January, p. 4; *Sandusky Register*, 21 September, p. 4.

1892. "[Humming birds obtained from a London museum]." *Sandusky Register*, 15 January, p. 4.

1893. "Our museum," pp. 128-131. *In Annual Report, The Board of Education of the City of Sandusky, Ohio for the School Year Ending August 31, 1893.* I. F. Mack & Bro., Sandusky, Ohio. 340 pp.

1895. "[Prof. Moseley and the superintendent of Sandusky Schools visited Mr. Tuttle's home to see taxidermy specimens for museum]." *Erie County Reporter*, 25 April, p. 4.

1896. "A rare treasure added to Professor Moseley's collection at the high school." *Sandusky Sunday Register*, 18 February, p. 1.

1896. "[Room change for museum]." *Sandusky Register*, 28 March, p. 8.

1901. "High school museum." *Sandusky Register*, 6 May, p. 8.

1901. "Largest and finest. In Ohio are some high school museum collections. Open to visitors. For one more Sunday—some of the interesting things to be shown by Prof. Moseley." *Sandusky Star-Journal,* 10 May, p. 4.

1903. "Fine collection added to the school museum. Rare specimens of plants and flowers and fish fossils collected by the late Herman Engels." *Sandusky Star-Journal*, 9 June, p. 3.

1904. "Our birds. Prof. Moseley's splendid museum in the high school—affords students rare opportunities to study them." *Sandusky Register,* 4 March, p. 3.

1905. "Growth of the high school museum." *The Fram,* [Sandusky High School] 4(7):3-6. May. **ELM**.

1905. "Our museum." *Sandusky Register,* 16 June, pp. 9-10. Carroll C. Page.

1906. "A nice fat boa con[strictor]. A shark's man-eating jaw, the sword from a sword fish and some Katzenjammer cockroaches are among the interesting things to be seen at the high school museum." *Sandusky Star-Journal,* 30 January, p. 2.

1906. "Big crowds at museum. Attendance has grown in past and still so continues. Last chance this year presents itself today. Department of curios authorized by act of city Board of Education and Advancement it has made during the five years of its existence—statistics given." *Sandusky Register,* 8 April, p. 4. (Reprinted under the title "The High School Museum." *In* Charles E. Frohman. *Sandusky Potpourri,* Item 67. The Ohio Historical Society, Columbus. 1974).

1906. "Adds to museum. Prof. Moseley secured fine specimens. In southern Europe. Also visited Morroco and Tanger and had an enjoyable and profitable summer—arrived home Tuesday." *Sandusky Star-Journal,* 6 September, p. 5.

1906. "New teachers are appointed ... Prof. Moseley donates to high school museum ..." *Sandusky Register,* 15 September, p. 5.

1907. "Many people visited high school museum. Was open for first time this year Sunday afternoon." *Sandusky Register,* 11 February, p. 3.

1907. "Chinese day at museum. Proceeds to be forwarded to Red-cross Society at Washington. Prof. Moseley's request granted by educators." ... *Sandusky Register,* 23 February, p. 2.

1907. "Ornithological treasures. Mr. Moseley receives from New York the most important addition to his bird collection that has been made for years." *Sandusky Register,* 4 March, p. 3.

1910. "The high school museum." *The Fram,* [Sandusky High School] 9(6):8-10, April. [Lee W. Sexton].

1911. "Interesting exhibits at our high school museum. Many visitors were astounded to find display occupies seven rooms—Prof. Moseley comments on economic botany specimens [basswood]." *Sandusky Register,* 10 March, p. 4. **ELM**.

1912.   "Many birds of many kinds in the high school museum. Inspection of collection shows nearly seven hundred exhibits, which public may view for last time this season, . . ." *Sandusky Register*, 12 March, p. 12. **ELM**.

1913.   "Deadly disease germs will be shown at high school museum. Prof. Moseley announces exhibition of unusual interest to the public, . . ." *Sandusky Register*, 11 April, p. 5.

1914.   "Records show surprising increase in high school museum attendance. Audience numbered seven persons, but average 2,000 annually—students at tribute causes lack of interest." *Sandusky Register*, 10 May, p. 4.

1915.   "Professor Moseley's part of high school museum may be lost." *Sandusky Star-Journal*, 7 April, p. 1.

1915.   "Moseley specimens stay at Sandusky high's big museum. Decision reached through generous agreement by Prof. Moseley. He will receive $200 per year as curator under contract." *Sandusky Star-Journal*, 10 April, p. 9.

1918.   "The value of a natural history museum." *Sandusky Register*, 1 June, p. 2. **ELM**.

1921.   "Sandusky high [school] museum now one of the best, is being made greater." *Sandusky Register*, 31 December, p. 20.

1924.   "Nearly 17,000 specimens in Sandusky High School museum. Prof. Moseley 35 years in the making fine collections. Founder of one of country's best school natural history museums urges fire proof building to house exhibits." *Sandusky Register*, 27 April, Section 2, p. 1.

1926.   "Moseley will exhibit rare Hawaiian birds at museum on Sunday." *Sandusky Register*, 4 December, p. 3.

1927.   "Prof. Moseley seeks to learn where skeleton at museum came from." *Sandusky Register*, 16 January, p. 8.

1927.   "[18]77 rattles skeleton." *Sandusky Register*, 30 January, p. 3. Paul B. Mason.

1927.   "High [school] museum has relic passenger pigeon days." *Sandusky Register*, 30 April, p. 3. **ELM**.

1928.   "Local museum to exhibit specimen of crocodile bird." *Sandusky Register*, 22 March, p. 5. **ELM**.

1928.   "Hummingbird collection is high [school] museum feature. Public invited to view 50 varities . . ." *Sandusky Register*, 24 March, p. 3.

1928. "Thousands of specimens at high [school] museum today; ... Prof. Moseley identifies strange lamper eel." *Sandusky Register*, 9 December, p. 10.

1929. "Moseley calls attention to some specimens at high school museum here." *Sandusky Register*, 2 March, p. 3.

1929. "Rare specimens of birds are on display at Museum . . ." *Sandusky Register*, 9 March, p. 3.

1930. "Woodchuck is one of specimens to be seen at Museum Sunday." *Sandusky Register*, 6 December, p. 7.

1931. "Dried specimens of lotus plant [*Nelumbo lutea*] to be shown at Museum Sunday." *Sandusky Register*, 18 April, p. 2. **ELM**.

1931. "Sandusky Museum open to public December 6th." *Bee Gee News*, 15(14): 4. 14 April; 16(11): 1, 4. 1 December.

1932. "Sandusky High [School] opens Museum." *Bee Gee News*, 16(21): 1. 23 February.

1932. "Local museum open today and many expected. Exhibits of fairy shrimps and live termites will be on display . . . at the high school museum under the direction of Prof. E. L. Moseley of Bowling Green State College." *Sandusky Regist*er, 6 March, p. 12.

1932. "High school museum may be moved from Sandusky." *Sandusky Star-Journal*, 3 December, p. 3.

1933. "Attic houses valuable museum. Offers much information of this region of Ohio. Few in country can equal quality of exhibits here." *Sandusky Register,* 6 August, p. 8.

1938. "Prof. Moseley's museum moved to [Bowling Green State] University. Sandusky High School loses collection of rare specimens long here." *Sandusky Star-Journal*, 2 July, p. 1.

1939. "Much hard work used to obtain noted local curio." *Sandusky Daily News*, 6 February, p. 1. Albert Gililland.

1978. "The Elderlies: Sandusky's pet rock [16 foot concretion]." *Sandusky Register*, 18 February, p. A-4. Karl Kurtz.

1984. "Stuffed exotic birds highlight showcases." *BG News*, 18 April, p. 3. Patti Skinner.

VI. List of Writings in Manuscript about Moseley by Ronald L. Stuckey   Archive No. 1035

1970.   Bibliography of Edwin Lincoln Moseley. 14 pp. Revised 1983. 20 pp. Typewritten.

1971.   Edwin Lincoln Moseley [Second part of a lecture presented to the Erie County Historical Society, 29 April 1971]. Handwritten. 4 pp.

1981.   Edwin Lincoln Moseley: [Prepared for Keir B. Sterling's "Biographical Dictionary of Naturalists]." 4 pp. Revised 1996. 5 pp. Typewritten. (Published, 1997; cited on page 67 of this book).

1983.   Edwin Lincoln Moseley's contributions to science, 18 pp. + Abstract published in the *Ohio Journal of Science* 83(2): 8-9. 1983. Manuscript 1 p.; [numbers of] books and articles published in scientific and popular journals, 1 p.; [list of] major publication(s) in each discipline, 1 p. Typewritten. (Published in chapter 9 of the book, *Edwin Lincoln Moseley (1865-1948): Naturalist, Scientist, Educator* by Niederhofer and Stuckey, 1998; cited on page 67 of this book).

1995.   Ronald L. Stuckey's interest in Edwin L. Moseley, 1 p. 26 October; plan for publication on book on the life and achievements of Edwin Lincoln Moseley, 3 pp. 11 November. Typewritten.

1995.   Relationship between Professor Edwin L. Moseley and his student, Norbert A. Lange, 1 p. 11 November. Typewritten. (with Relda E. Niederhofer).

1997.   The Lange Trust: Norbert A. Lange (1892-1970), Marion C. Lange (1898-1975), 2 pp. Typewritten.

1997.   Drought in 2037: Forecasted by Edwin L. Moseley. *Ohio Journal of Science* 97(2): A24. [Abstract]. Manuscript. 1 p. Typewritten. Notes and + 12 illustrations used for presentation.

1997.   [A list of] extensively quoted passages from publications by Bowling Green State University in the Moseley book, 1 p. Typewritten. (with Relda E. Niederhofer).

1997.   List of photographs used in the Moseley book by Niederhofer and Stuckey (1998), 4 pp., 6 pp. Typewritten. (with Relda E. Niederhofer).

1997.   A numbered list of photographs and their captions as used in the Moseley book by Niederhofer and Stuckey (1998), 14 pp. July 1998; revised and reformatted. 8 pp. Typewritten. (with Relda E. Niederhofer).

Edwin Lincoln Moseley (1865-1948)
Professor of Biological Sciences, Bowling Green Normal College.

(Taken in the early 1920's; "Edwin Lincoln Moseley Papers," MS-87,
Center for Archival Collections, BGSU, Bowling Green, Ohio)

Biographical Sources

I. Sketches, Commentaries, Stories   Archive No. 1001

1898. "Prof. Moseley's new position. Toledo Board of Education makes him an offer." *Sandusky Register*, 1 July, p. 5; *Sandusky Weekly Register*, 6 July, p. 12.

1900. "[Prof. Moseley hosts merry party for Sandusky High School graduates attending or about to attend college]." *Sandusky Register*, 13 August, p. 2.

1910. Edwin Lincoln Moseley, p. 336. *In* American Men of Science, ed. 2: 336.

1914. "G. R. Thorpe will probably be chosen to succeed Prof. E. L. Moseley as teacher of science." *Sandusky Star-Journal*, 17 June, p. 4.

1914. "Prof. E. L. Moseley, noted teacher of science leaves Sandusky High. Will resign to accept professorship in new State Normal School at Bowling Green—Teacher here for 25 years—built up great Museum." *Sandusky Register*, 17 June, pp. 1, 13.

1914. "Tribute paid to Professor E. L. Moseley who leaves local school work." *Sandusky Star-Journal*, 19 June, p.14. Roy E. Offenhauer.

1916. Prof. Moseley named to Bowling Green's City Health Board. *Sandusky Star-Journal*, 12 January 1916, p. 1.

1917. Edwin Lincoln Moseley, pp. 269-270. *In The Ohio Blue Book, or Who's Who in the Buckeye State: A Cyclopedia of Biography of Men and Women in Ohio.* Charles Summer Van Tassel, Toledo, Ohio. 479 pp. C. S. Van Tassel, ed.

1923. "Moseley is man of many biological discoveries" *Sandusky Register*, 8 December, p. 3.

Bibliography of Writings By Edwin Lincoln Moseley

1929. In 50 years, E. L. Moseley hasn't missed a day from class through illness. *Sandusky Register*, 21 July, p. 5.

1934. Moseley, scientist who won Ripley mention, Akron guest. He's added another year to record set in cartoon. 14 June, p. _ [Newspaper not identified].

1936. "Bowling Green Professor hasn't missed class in 50 years because of illness. Took time out for journeys to far places." *Toledo Sunday Times*, 10 May 1936, p. 9.

1937. "Prof. E. L. Moseley wins plaudits of his admirers at a birthday dinner." *Daily Sentinel-Tribune*, Bowling Green. 31 March, p. 4. (Also *Sandusky Register*, 4 April, p. 11). [Ivan E. Lake].

1937. "Biographical sketch of Prof. Edwin L. Moseley." *Daily Sentinel-Tribune*, Bowling Green. 31 March, p. 5. [Ivan E. Lake].

1937. "Professor Emeritus of Biology." *Bee Gee News* 21(26): 1. 31 March.

1937. "Dr. Williams lauds Moseley: Teacher, author, scientist honored this week." *Bee Gee News* 21(26): 1, 2, 4. 31 March. Homer B. Williams.

1937. "Banquet for E. L. Moseley." *Bee Gee News* 21 (26): 1. 31 March.

1943. University honors Moseley, . . . Honorary degrees to be given Aug. 13. [Newspaper not identified].

1943. "Prof. Moseley to receive honors at Bowling Green." *Sandusky Register Star-News*, 19 July, p. 10.

1943. Long-range weather man. An Ohio scientist with a remarkable record of accuracy, gives C. G. readers a forecast of dry and wet periods in years ahead. *Country Gentleman*, 113(11): 12, 38, 40. November. Moran Tudury.

1945. Edwin Lincoln Moseley: The biography of an educator. *Nature Magazine* 38:37-39. January. Josephine True.

1946. "Sixty-two years ago, William W. Lathrop and Edwin L. Moseley roomed in the same house while attending the University." *The Michigan Alumnus*, 23 November, p. 141.

1948. "Dr. E. L. Moseley is ill in Dayton. *Daily Sentinel-Tribune*, Bowling Green, 3 May, p. 1.

1948. "Bowling Green scientist's condition reported better. Dr. E. L. Moseley, noted for long-range weather forecasts, is ill in Dayton." 4 May, p. _. [Newspaper not identified].

1948. "Say Dr. Moseley's condition improves." *Sandusky Register Star-News*, 4 May, p. 8.

1948. "Dr. E. L. Moseley's life one of great achievements. Research into many fields of science featured his long life." *Daily Sentinel-Tribune*, Bowling Green. 7 June 1948, p. 2. [Ivan E. Lake].

1948. "Moseley's admirers saddened by his death; praised as a genius and humanitarian." *Daily Sentinel-Tribune*, Bowling Green. 8 June 1948.

1948? "Dr. Moseley's accomplishments." *Sandusky Register Star-News* [Date not known]. p. 4.

1948. "The passing show. [Last photograph of Moseley taken by Dr. Kelley Hale used on cover of June 1948 issue of the *Bowling Green State University Alumni Magazine*]." *News-Journal*, Wilmington. 24 July, p. 1. I. C. Clinton.

1948. "Moseley career lauded by President of BGSU. Influence of deceased professor-botanist will continue, Dr. Prout tells Kiwanians." *Toledo Blade*, 10 September, p. 29.

1949. "Ohio Story will dramatize work of Dr. Moseley." *Sandusky Register Star-News*, 3 March, p. 13.

1949-1950. Dr. Moseley, friend, teacher and naturalist. *Toledo Naturalists Association Annual Bulletin*. 1949-1950, pp.12-13. Seymour VanGundy.

1952. Edwin Lincoln Moseley, 1865-1948: A Bibliography Manuscript. Typewritten. 3 pp. Hubert Porter Stone.

1956. Edwin Lincoln Moseley. p. 159. *In National Cyclopaedia of American Biography* . . . Vol. 41. James T. White & Co., New York. 1956, 611 pp. + Index.

1958. "Zion Couples Clubs: Hears Dr. Frank Prout's tribute to former SHS faculty member." *Sandusky Register*, 25 September, p. 8.

1959. "Memorial for E. L. Moseley on April 14." *Sandusky Register*, 3 April, pp. 1, 8.

1959. "Memorial Services at Sandusky High Honor Dr. Edwin L. Moseley. *Sandusky Register*, 14 April, p. 1.

1959. "The inquiring mind of Mr. Moseley." *Bowling Green State University Magazine.* 4(4):16-20, November. Frank Jay Prout.

1959. "Channel finally named for Dr. Moseley." *Sandusky Register*, 21 December, p. 7.

1960. "Sandusky outer channel named for Moseley." *Bowling Green State University Magazine* 5(1):22. February.

1967. [Edwin Lincoln Moseley], pp. 28, 29, 94, 130, 209, 210-211. *In. The History of Bowling Green State University.* Bowling Green State University Press, Bowling Green, Ohio. 234 pp. James Robert Overman.

1971. "Professor Moseley. *In* Charles H. Frohman. *Sandusky's 3rd Dimension.* Item 80. Ohio Historical Society, Columbus. (Reprinted, pp. 61-64. *In Edwin Lincoln Moseley. Lake Erie, Floods, Lake Levels, Northeast Storms. The Formation of Sandusky Bay and Cedar Point.* Ohio Historical Society, Columbus. 1973. 64 pp.).

1972. "The legend and legacy of a farsighted professor." *Toledo Blade Sunday Magazine.* 1972, 9 April. pp. 20, 21, 23, 24. Don Wolfe.

1974. "Dr. Moseley: The eccentric professor. He taught some courses in English, Latin, and geometry, but science was his forte. In fact, for many years he was the entire science department." *At Bowling Green, News for Alumni* 4(6):15-16 December. Randy Morrison.

1980. "1880 Union City graduate achieves success as a professor at Bowling Green University." *Coldwater Daily Reporter*, Coldwater, Michigan, 9 July, p. 3. Mary Alaniz.

1981. "The elderlies: Sandusky's Professor Moseley." *Sandusky Register*, 8 November, p. A-4. Wilbert Ohlemacher.

1981. "The elderlies: More about Moseley." *Sandusky Register*, 6 December, p. A-4. Wilbert Ohlemacher.

1982. "The elderlies: Learning science the Moseley way," *Sunday Sandusky Register*, 31 January, p. A-4. Wilbert Ohlemacher.

1983. "The elderlies: Successful Sandusky graduates." *Sandusky Register*, 16 January, p. A-4. Wilbert Ohlemacher.

1983. Edwin L. Moseley, internationally known naturalist, as viewed by those who knew him. *Ohio Journal of Science* 83(2):8. Abstract. Relda E. Niederhofer.

1983. Edwin Lincoln Moseley's contributions to science. *Ohio Journal of Science* 83(2):8-9. Abstract. Ronald L. Stuckey.

1984. "Sandusky revisited: BG instructor [Relda E. Niederhofer] finds interesting facts on Professor Moseley." *Sandusky Register*, 19 February, p. A-4. Wilbert Ohlemacher.

1984. "Moseley contributed more than funds to BGSU." *BG News*, 23 October, p. 5. Jim Nieman.

1984. Edwin Lincoln Moseley: Naturalist and teacher, 1865-1948. *Northwest Ohio Quarterly* 56(1):3-17, winter. Harold E. Mayfield.

1985. "Edwin Moseley: BG's eccentric scientist." *Daily Sentinel-Tribune*, Bowling Green. 23 August, p. A-11. Jim Nieman.

1985. "Edwin Lincoln Moseley: An internationally known scientist, a locally known eccentric." *At Bowling Green* [an alumni magazine] 14(4):4, winter. Relda E. Niederhofer.

1988. Edwin Lincoln Moseley: An internationally known naturalist. *Bartonia* 54:74-82. Relda E. Niederhofer.

1989. "Moseley's inspiration knew few bounds." *Sandusky Register*, 13 August, pp. B1, 2, 5. Relda E. Niederhofer.

1989. "Opinion. Learning about learning from Moseley's example." *Sandusky Register*, 21 August p. A-4. Robert E. Pifer, ed.

1997. Edwin Lincoln Moseley, pp. 559-561. *In* Keir B. Sterling, Richard P. Harmond, George A. Cevasco, and Lorne F. Hammond. *Biographical Dictionary of American and Canadian Naturalists and Environmentalists*. Greenwood Press, Westport, Connecticut. xix, 937. Ronald L. Stuckey.

1998. *Edwin Lincoln Moseley (1865-1948): Naturalist, Scientist, Educator*. RLS Creations, Columbus, Ohio. xxvi, 292 pp. Relda E. Niederhofer and Ronald L. Stuckey. (Reviews: *Ohio Journal of Science* 100(2): 28-29. 2000; *Plant Science Bulletin* 45(2): 52-53. 1999; *Taxon* 48(4): 889-890. 1999).

II. Obituaries   Archive No. 1023

1948. "Dr. Moseley dead at Bowling Green. Was famous for long range weather forecasts." *Advertiser-Tribune*, Tiffin. 7 June, p. 4.

1948. "Dr. Moseley dies at Bowling Green. University's noted predictor of droughts was 83." *Cleveland Plain Dealer,* 7 June, p. 8.

1948. "Dr. Moseley, eminent B.G.U. scientist, dies. Passes away quietly Sunday to bring close to 34 years at local campus." *Daily Sentinel-Tribune*, Bowling Green. 7 June, p. 1. [Ivan E. Lake].

1948. "Dr. E. L. Moseley's life one of great achievements. Research into many fields of science featured his long life." *Daily Sentinel-Tribune*, Bowling Green. 7 June, p. 2. [Ivan E. Lake].

1948. "Bowling Green scientist dies. Dr. Edwin Moseley, 83, ill five weeks; career traced." *Fremont News-Messenger,* 7 June, p. 3.

1948. "Dr. Edwin Lincoln Moseley." *Michigan Alumnus*, 9 October, p. 28.

1948. "Dr. Edwin Moseley, weather authority." *New York Times*, 7 June, p. 4.

1948. "Dr. Moseley, 83, dies and services at Bowling Green." *Sandusky Star Register Star-News*, 7 June, pp. 1, 10.

1948. "Amplify organ music during Moseley rites. *Sandusky Register Star-News*, 8 June, p. 1; also *Fremont News-Messenger*, 8 June, p. 2; *Advertiser-Tribune*, Tiffin. 8 June, p. 14. (Based on News Release, B.G.S.U., 8 June 1948. Typewritten, 1 p. Paul W. Jones).

1948. "Noted scientist: Dr. Moseley. Retired member of BGSU faculty." *Toledo Blade*, 7 June, p. 1.

1948. "Dr. Moseley's scientific findings has wide range. BGSU educator best known for extended weather forecasts based on tree growth." *Toledo Blade*, 7 June, p. 24.

1948. "Dr. Edwin Moseley, BGU. scientist, dies. Acclaim won for system of predicting periods of floods, drought." *Toledo Times*, 7 June, pp. 1, 2.

1948. "'Pete' Moseley gone, but not forgotten." *Toledo Times,* 13 June, p. 2-x; *Toledo Naturalists Association Bulletin* 2(10):[1]. July and August; "Dr. Moseley gone, but not forgotten." *Ohio Conservation Bulletin* 12(8):15. August. Lou Campbell.

1948. "Prof. Moseley, famed weather student, dies." *News Journal*, Wilmington, Ohio. 7 June, p. 1.

III. Will and Estate Archive No. 1024

1948. "Moseley estate to aid students. Scholarship trust fund set up by will." *Advertiser-Tribune*, Tiffin. 10 June, p. 4.

1948. "Moseley's estate to total $80,000. Preliminary inventory is filed in court." *Advertiser-Tribune*, Tiffin. 21 June, p. 2.

1948. "Journalism student given Moseley Award." *Advertiser-Tribune*, Tiffin, 22 June, p. 7.

1948. "Dr. Moseley wills his estate to aid worthy students." *Daily Sentinel-Tribune*, Bowling Green, 9 June, pp. 1, 2.

1948. "Dr. Moseley's rich legacy." *Daily Sentinel-Tribune*, Bowling Green, 10 June, p. 4.

1948. "Will sets up student fund. Moseley leaves $100,000 in trust for Bowling Green enrollees." *Fremont News-Messenger*, 10 June, p. 10.

1948. "Select recipient for Moseley's Scholarship." *Sandusky Register Star-News*, 22 June, p. 3.

1948. "Moseley estate will benefit worthy students. Bowling Green State University President named in will." *Toledo Blade*, 10 June, p. 1.

1948. "Berkey girl awarded Moseley Scholarship. Journalism student at BGSU recipient of first benefit under scientist's will. *Toledo Blade*, 22 June, p. _. [Not located in the newspaper].

1948. "$100,000 for scholars. Moseley will sets up student trust fund." *Toledo Times*, 10 June, pp. 1,4.

Obituaries (Continued from page 68)

1948. Edwin Lincoln Moseley. *Science* 107:645.

1948. Edwin Lincoln Moseley. *Wilson Bulletin* 60(3):191.

1949. Edwin Lincoln Moseley. *Ohio Journal of Science* 49:168. Charles H. Otis.

1950. Edwin Lincoln Moseley. *The Auk* 67(4):549-550. T. S. Palmer.

In the Library of the Hayes Presidential Center

Ronald L. Stuckey and Nan Card, Curator of Manuscripts, viewing archival items pertaining to this book, *Bibliography and Archival Guide to the Writings of Edwin Lincoln Moseley*, in the Library of the Hayes Presidential Center, Fremont, Ohio.

(Taken 16 April 2002 by Gil Gonzalez for RLS)

GUIDE TO ARCHIVES

I. Archives for the Book, *Edwin Lincoln Moseley (1865-1948), Naturalist, Scientist, Educator* (1998), by Relda E. Niederhofer and Ronald L. Stuckey (Archive Nos. 1000-1099)

Deposited in the Hayes Presidential Center, Fremont, Ohio. Donated 4 June 1999; 10 January 2002.

1000   Introduction and Guide to the Moseley Archives Assembled by Ronald L. Stuckey

1001   Biographical Sketches of Edwin L. Moseley.

1002   Foreword; Guy L. Denny.

1003   Preface; Relda E. Niederhofer, biographical.

1004   Preface; Ronald L. Stuckey, biographical.

1005   Dedication to T. Richard Fisher, biographical.

1006   Introduction; Chronology of Moseley's Life.

1007   Sandusky High School.

1008   Bowling Green State University.

1009   Chapter 1   Educator of Many Students [1945]; Josephine True.

1010   Chapter 2   Formative Years in Michigan; Union City High School; Steere Expedition to the Philippines (1887); High School Graduation Oration (1880).

1011	Chapter 3	Lauded by University President [1937]; Homer B. Williams; Roy E. Offenhauer.
1012	Chapter 4	The Inquiring Mind of a Teaching Scientist [1959]; Frank J. Prout.
1013	Chapter 5	Interviews with Students and Friends; Names of Individuals Interviewed.

          Lelia Bittikofer   Wilbert Ohlemacher
          Howard Braithwaite   Helen Ohlemacher
          Clarence Clark   Cynthia (Otis) Witte
          Ralph Dexter   Charles Otis
          Lewis Hause   Edna Scheid
          Ruth (Milkey) Holzhauser Louis Schultz, Sr.
          Inez (Reinheimer) Koch   Hazel Stockdale
          Ervin Kreischer   Rose (Steiner) Tschantz
          Claire Martin   Anonymous

1014	Chapter 6	Field Excursions for Moseley's Classes; List of Botany Field Excursions with date and place; Ralph H. McKelvey.
1015	Chapter 7	Family History: Moseley Family; Bingham Family.
1016	Chapter 8	Recollections of a Contemporary Naturalist [1981]; Milton B. Trautman.
1017	Chapter 9	Scientific Presentations and Publications; Numbers and Years of Moseley's Publications for Each Discipline; Presentations at Scientific Meetings; Contributions to Botany, Geology; Medical Science (Milk Sickness); Zoology; Membership in Professional Scientific Organizations; Numbers of Publications in Periodicals.
1018	Chapter 10	Forecasting Long-Range Weather Conditions; Predictions of Water Levels of Lake Erie; Table of Years When Trees Had Wide or Narrow Growth Rings; Moran Tudury; Evaluation of Moseley's Rainfall Predictions.
1019	Chapter 11	Books and Science Education; Trees, Stars, and Birds (1919); Our Wild Animals (1927); Other Worlds (1933); Field Trip and Classroom Incidents; Evaluation as a Teacher; Ivan E. "Doc" Lake.
1020	Chapter 12	The High School Museum; Large Concretion Unusual Artifact.

1021 Chapter 13 Selected Letters from Moseley's Correspondence; Letters Published Written to Miss Ione R. Pratt; Stella M. Horn, Raymond C. Osburn; Mr. and Mrs. Robert Van Gundy; J. LeRoy Weier; Mrs. Ellen Drewson; and others not published in the book.

1022 Chapter 14 Sandusky's Scientific and Economic Advantages; Edwin L. Moseley; Attractions for a Scientist in Geology, Botany, Zoology; Places of Interest-Castalia Prairie, Blue Hole Springs, Shorelines of Glacial Lakes, Sink Holes South of Castalia, Natural Resources; List of Lectures at the Sandusky High School.

1023 Chapter 15 Illness, Death, and Funeral; Letter of Niece, Pearl Ideler; Obituaries of Edwin L. Moseley.

1024 Chapter 16 Estate Trust Fund of Benefit to Students; Will of Edwin L. Moseley; Commentary on Will by Daily Sentinel-Tribune Editor, Spencer A. Canary.

1025 Chapter 17 Tributes from Former Students; Donald M. Love; R. E. Dillery; Seymour Van Gundy; Richard S. Phillips; List and Publication Source of Students who Assisted Moseley in his Research Projects.

1026 Chapter 18 Commentaries by Natural Science Writers; Louis W. Campbell; Roger Conant; Harold F. Mayfield.

1027 Chapter 19 Commemorated in Names; Plants-Solidago moseleyi, Thalictrum moseleyi; Fish-Gonorhynchus moseleyi; Bird-Actenoides moseleyi; Places-Moseley Hall; Moseley Channel.

1028 Chapter 20 Recognitions and Tributes; Honors and Recognitions while living, including Honorary Degree of Doctor of Humane Letters from Bowling Green State University (1943); Memorials and Tributes after his death, including those presented on several occasions by Bowling Green State University President Frank J. Prout; Moseley's Contributions to Sandusky and Bowling Green State University recognized in newspaper articles.

1029 Index by Charles E. Frohman to Moseley's Articles published in the Sandusky and Erie County Newspapers.

1030 Publication Notes; Libraries Consulted; Photograph and Archive Credits.

1031 Acknowledgments.

BIBLIOGRAPHY OF WRITINGS BY EDWIN LINCOLN MOSELEY

1032   Final Book Manuscript with copies of photographs used by printer.

1033   Final Book Manuscript which the printer photographed and used to print the book.

1034   Manuscripts and Publications about Moseley by Relda E. Niederhofer.

1035   Manuscripts and Publications about Moseley by Ronald L. Stuckey.

1036   Advertising Information.

1037   Moseley's Essays on Travels and on Other Topics.

1038   Moseley's Opinions, Editorials.

1039   Moseley's Lectures.

1040   Signed Permissions to publish quoted items and photographs in the book.

1041   Correspondence and Papers Pertaining to the Lange Trust, Sandusky, Ohio.

1042   Correspondence and Papers Pertaining to the Frost-Parker Foundation, Sandusky, Ohio.

1043   Correspondence and Papers Pertaining to the Printing of the Book by Thomson-Shore, Inc., Dexter, Michigan.

1044   Commentaries and reviews of the Moseley book.

1045   Ricki C. Herdendorf, financial papers.

1046   A Checklist of Ohio Species in Moseley's Herbarium, Compiled by Nathan William Easterly. Typewritten. 77 pp. [Original in Bowling Green State University Archives; copy to Dr. Anton A. Reznicek, University of Michigan Herbarium, 17 April 2000].

1047   Correspondence between Relda E. Niederhofer and Ronald L. Stuckey.

1048   Correspondence between Charles Middleton, Provost at Bowling Green State University and Ronald L. Stuckey.

1049   Correspondence of Ronald L. Stuckey with various individuals pertaining to this Moseley book project.

1050	Correspondence of Ronald L. Stuckey with various individuals who knew Professor Moseley or who worked at Bowling Green State University.
1051	Correspondence with Erie County Historical Society.
1052	Photographs and "Xerox" Copies of Photographs used in the Moseley Book by REN and RLS.
1053	Photographs and "Xerox" Copies of Photographs not used in the Moseley Book.
1054-1059	[Blank Numbers]
1060	Publications in Astronomy.
1061	Publications in Botany.
1062	Publications in Geology.
1063	Publications on Health and Hygiene (not used in Moseley book)
1064	Publications in Medical Science (Milk Sickness)
1065	Publications in Meteorology
1066	Publications in Ornithology
1067	Publications in Science Education and General Science
1068	Publications in Zoology.
1069	Students and Associates.
1070	Titles of Papers Presented at Meetings of the Ohio Academy of Science; also those that were published.
1071	List of Moseley's Reports as Secretary of the Ohio Academy of Science (1895-1904), including some reports.
1072	Titles of Papers Presented at Meetings of the Michigan Academy of Science, Arts, and Letters.
1073	Titles of Papers Presented at Meetings of Other Organizations.
1074-1099	[Blank Numbers]

II. Biographical Sources of Individuals in the Archives for the Book, *Edwin Lincoln Moseley (1865-1948), Naturalist, Scientist, Educator* by Relda E. Niederhofer and Ronald L. Stuckey

Name (Birth and Death Years)	Archive No.
Alice L. (Shuey) Baldosser (1913-1994)	1019
Bingham Family Genealogy	1015
Lelia Bittikofer (1889-1992)	1013
Howard Braithwaite (1913-)	1013
Louis W. Campbell (1889-1998)	1026
Clarence Clark (1912-)	1013
Roger Conant (1909-)	1026
Guy L. Denny (1944-)	1002
Ralph W. Dexter (1912–1991)	1013
R. E. Dillery	1025
Alyce (Myers) Oder-Doss (- 1999)	1019
Ellen Drewson	1021
T. Richard Fisher (1921-2000)	1005
Charles E. Frohman (1901-1976)	1029
Lewis Hause (1904-1984)	1013
Ruth (Milkey) Holzhauser (1908-1997)	1013
Stella M. Horn (- 1993)	1021
Inez (Reinheimer) Koch (1894-1986)	1013
Ervin Kreischer (1906-1986)	1013
Ivan E. "Doc" Lake (1901-1967)	1019
Norbert A. Lange (1892-1970)	1035
Marion C. Lange (1898-1975)	1035
Donald M. Love (1894-1974)	1025

Clare Martin (1888-1982)	**1013**
Harold F. Mayfield (1911-)	**1026**
Ralph H. McKelvey (1877-1957)	**1014**
Edwin L. Moseley (1865-1948)	**1001, 1006**
Moseley Family Genealogy	**1015**
Relda E. Niederhofer (1928-)	**1003**
Roy E. Offenhauer (1891-1938)	**1011**
Helen Ohlemacher (1895-1987)	**1013**
Wilbert Ohlemacher (1892-1987)	**1013**
Charles Otis (1886-1979)	**1013**
Richard S. Phillips (1913-1993)	**1025**
Ione R. Pratt	**1021**
Frank J. Prout (1883-1967)	**1012**
Grace (Myers) Ohl-Miller-Ruth (1905-2001)	**1019**
Edna Scheid (1890-1990)	**1013**
Louis Schultz, Sr. (1882-1969)	**1013**
Hazel Stockdale (1893-1989)	**1013**
Leora I. (Shuey) Stuckey (1903-1966)	**1019**
Ronald L. Stuckey (1938-)	**1004**
Milton B. Trautman (1899-1991)	**1016**
Josephine True	**1009**
Rose (Steiner) Tschantz (1905-1993)	**1013**
Moran Tudury	**1018**
Robert Van Gundy	**1021**
Seymour Van Gundy (1931-)	**1025**
J. LeRoy Weier (1888-1971)	**1021**
Homer B. Williams (1865-1943)	**1011**
Cynthia (Otis) Witte	**1013**

Edwin Lincoln Moseley (1865-1948)
Professor Emeritus of Biology, Bowling Green State University.

(Taken at an advanced age, "Edwin Lincoln Moseley Papers," MS-87,
Center for Archival Collections, BGSU, Bowling Green, Ohio)

A Biographical Sketch

Ivan E. Lake

Early in life, Edwin Lincoln Moseley realized that he was not of an ordinary family, but a lineage of which he was always to be proud. Born 29 March 1865, 11 days before the end of the Civil War, in Union City, Branch County, Michigan, his parents were William A. and Sophia (Bingham) Moseley. His father was a native of Westfield, Massachusetts, and his mother was the first white child born in Honolulu and the second white child born in the Hawaiian Islands. Her father, Hiram Bingham, was the first missionary to the Islands.

Moseley's uncle of the second generation, another Hiram Bingham, went as a missionary to the Gilbert Islands, 2,000 miles west of the Hawaiian Islands and he, with the aid of his courageous wife, translated the entire Bible into the Gilbertese language. When it was put into type, he traveled to New York City to read proof personally on the book. Hiram Bingham of the third generation, a cousin of Moseley, is the present Senator from Massachusetts. Moseley was the youngest of nine children; he had four brothers and four sisters.

Life as a Student

Early in life Moseley showed signs of being a fine student, and before he was old enough to read he was able to count up to a very high number. Merchants in his home town often asked him to solve problems which puzzled them, and his family envisioned the time when he possibly would be a professor of mathematics. He quickly showed a tremendous curiosity for learning and at the age of 15 graduated in 1810 from Union City High School. Being too young for admission to The University of Michigan, he spent a fifth year in high school doing research, and then entered The University. After four years he graduated in 1885 with such a conspicuous record of scholarship and achievement that he was the youngest of 83 graduates and one of two students to be awarded the Master of Arts degree in this short time span.

Moseley quickly learned to be thrifty and was able to learn many tasks for himself, including selling magazines and eventually purchasing a fine foot-powered saw with which he fashioned brackets and photograph frames. He gained the distinction of not only completing his courses, but also was always proud of the fact that he earned his way through the University. With an exception of $150, he was able to live on no more than 50 cents per week by doing his own cooking.

Expedition to the Philippines

A teaching position at Grand Rapids, Michigan, occupied his time during the next two years, but in 1887 a golden opportunity came to him when Joseph B. Steere of The University of Michigan invited him to go on a scientific expedition to study on the Philippine Islands. The group visited nearly every part of the Archipelago, making large collections of birds, shells, and corals. Many species not previously known to science were discovered. While studying there, he gathered much of the material which formed the nucleus of the Sandusky High School and later Bowling Green State University museums. A year was spent in the islands and in Japan and China, during which time he gathered much very valuable data to contribute to science. When his research there ended, Moseley returned to Michigan, where he spent a year tutoring private students, and during his leisure he read the entire Gospel of Matthew in the original form.

Science Teacher at Sandusky

An opening for a science teacher at Sandusky, Ohio, gave Moseley an opportunity to join the faculty of the High School there in 1889, where he taught for the next 25 years. He gained a wide reputation as a scientist of great ability, and established a museum which was probably the finest high school museum of natural history in the United States and possibly in the world. For a while he taught Geometry, and during that time discovered an original method of teaching the Pythagorean proposition. He spent a great deal of time in the study of and research into the formation of Sandusky Bay and Cedar Point, later publishing the results of his findings. That study proved to be most valuable and has been read in many countries, even Russia, where it was useful in science.

Teaching at Bowling Green School

Moseley conducted his various researches into wild life, becoming a fine authority on water life and particularly on the water life in the region of Sandusky. For years he worked on the faculty with Homer B. Williams, then Superintendent of the Sandusky schools. When Williams accepted the invitation of the Board of

Trustees of the newly established Bowling Green State Normal School in 1912, the latter began considering his faculty. In 1914 classes were opened; Moseley was one of the teachers. He taught under great handicaps during that first year when classes were in the Armory and laboratory periods were in the high school building, the present Junior High School. Three days of his time were spent in Bowling Green teaching and the other three days he was in Toledo with classes there in the Toledo branch of the institution.

The transfer of classes to the new Administration building and the early expansion to the new Science building found the science classes having a rapid increase in size. Moseley's classroom burden showed a similar increase, but he maintained his work at a high level always. Not until 1923 when Clare S. Martin was appointed to the faculty, did a division in classroom responsibilities come, at which time the latter took over the physical sciences, and Moseley devoted his time to the biological courses, which were his preference.

For 22 years Moseley taught classes on the Bowling Green campus, and during that time his daily life and educational activities at the University became so much a part of the place that his name became traditionally a part of the institution. Between 5,500 and 6,000 students are estimated to have benefited from his teaching during the time that he guided classes in the high schools and local university. But though he was a teacher for 51 years, Moseley never ceased to be a student. Always a diligent investigator of every part of the field of natural history, he spent years of his life studying and recording the facts in order that others might profit from the findings that he made. (From Ivan E. Lake, 1937; see page 64 for citation).

Long Range Weather Forecasts

The most widespread publicity came to Moseley late in life when, following his retirement in 1936, he spent a vast amount of time in the study of old weather records and their relationship with sunspot cycles. He then advanced his theory of recurring periods of wet and dry weather every 90.4 years.

Moseley bravely ventured his reputation by freely forecasting the weather far in advance, and in the last 12 years he established a remarkable record of accuracy in predicting periods of heavy rain and floods and others of drought. His latest prediction early in January forecast 1948 and 1949 as "wet" years, and he declared that 1950 will be a dry year in the middle west. His research did not attempt to cover the entire United States but was confined to areas from Western Pennsylvania to eastern Kansas, including about 15 states.

Moseley pointed out that magnetic conditions on the earth and on the sun average about the same every 22.6 years. The position of the moon and other planets, which affect the abundance of spots on the sun, is very nearly the same every fourth cycle, or 90.4 years, he declared. Moseley reached the conclusion that every 90.4 years the weather would be relatively the same and that if he could establish the amount of rainfall through past records, he could predict with reasonable accuracy just what the rainfall would approximate 90.4 years after that particular period.

Research was Thorough

Moseley's research was hampered by the fact that many areas of the country had no weather stations to make records back that many years, and so he turned to ancient trees to confirm his theory in part. Trees grow rapidly in wet periods and more slowly in times of drought. Growth is indicated by the width of annual tree rings, and by measuring the rings of trees, after establishing the exact year in which the tree was cut down, he could determine periods of wet and dry conditions.

Moseley collected cross sections of about 300 trees that grew in this part of the United States and these, together with those actual weather station figures as were available, gave him the information about past wet and dry years that he wanted. He then would figure out the kind of weather ahead for many years.

Few weather records go back as far as 100 years today, but Moseley recently pointed out that four of the three cross-sections in his possession (two Hemlocks in Western Pennsylvania and two white oaks in Ohio) began to grow while Christopher Columbus was still living. He observed that each of the four showed a very narrow ring for 1494, indicating that that year was a very dry year. He counted out ninety and ninety-one years later to show that those rings were also very narrow and the rings at each of similar intervals after that are also very narrow, substantially proving his point of repetition of a drought period each 90.4 years.

Predicts Drought in 2037

Observing that he had foreseen the general drought conditions which had come in 1946-1947, he recently predicted that the year 2037 will be a dry one. Moseley was admittedly far from thorough with his weather cycle research at the time of his death. He granted that successful prediction based on his limited research was greatly restricted, but he was convinced that his research would provide other scientists with information that would help guide them to discoveries that would increase present knowledge of the subject.

Lake Shore Sinking

Another discovery, not so greatly publicized, came from Moseley's research, which interests inhabitants along the southern shore of Lake Erie. Moseley learned that Cedar Point and the southern shore of Lake Erie have been sinking at a rate of 2.14 feet each hundred years. He pointed out that during the long ages back, the islands of Lake Erie were a part of the mainland. Lake shore erosion specialists have found Moseley's study of that region to be of great benefit to them.

None of the members of Moseley's immediate family survive. He leaves a number of nieces and nephews, but his largest "family" is the vast body of former students, many of whom he financed through college himself, all of whom gained great benefit from his careful teaching, his constant demand for accuracy, and his great example in increasingly seeking new scientific information. (From Ivan E. Lake, 1948; see page 65 for citation).

Tombstone in Oak Grove Cemetery, Bowling Green, Ohio.

(Taken 5 April 1997 by Ronald L. Stuckey)

DATE DUE

PRINTED IN U.S.A.